Christopher H. Skinner,
Editor

M000318003

Single-Subject Designs
for School Psychologists

Single-Subject Designs for School Psychologists has been co-published simultaneously as *Journal of Applied School Psychology*, Volume 20, Number 2 2004.

Pre-publication
REVIEWS,
COMMENTARIES,
EVALUATIONS . . .

"This book is exactly what is needed to promote evidence-based practice. IN THIS AGE OF ACCOUNTABILITY, IT SHOULD BE ON THE DESK OF EVERY SCHOOL PSYCHOLOGIST."

Jeff Sigafoos, PhD
Professor
Department of Special Education
The University of Texas at Austin

The Haworth Press, Inc.

Single-Subject Designs
for School Psychologists

Single-Subject Designs for School Psychologists has been co-published simultaneously as *Journal of Applied School Psychology*, Volume 20, Number 2 2004.

The *Journal of Applied School Psychology*™ *(formerly Special Services in the Schools)** Monographic "Separates"

Below is a list of "separates," which in serials librarianship means a special issue simultaneously published as a special journal issue or double-issue *and* as a "separate" hardbound monograph. (This is a format which we also call a "DocuSerial.")

"Separates" are published because specialized libraries or professionals may wish to purchase a specific thematic issue by itself in a format which can be separately cataloged and shelved, as opposed to purchasing the journal on an on-going basis. Faculty members may also more easily consider a "separate" for classroom adoption.

"Separates" are carefully classified separately with the major book jobbers so that the journal tie-in can be noted on new book order slips to avoid duplicate purchasing.

You may wish to visit Haworth's website at . . .

http://www.HaworthPress.com

. . . to search our online catalog for complete tables of contents of these separates and related publications.

You may also call 1-800-HAWORTH (outside US/Canada: 607-722-5857), or Fax 1-800-895-0582 (outside US/Canada: 607-771-0012), or e-mail at:

docdelivery@haworthpress.com

Single-Subject Designs for School Psychologists, edited by Christopher H. Skinner, PhD (Vol. 20, No. 2, 2004). *"This book is exactly what is needed to promote evidence-based practice. IN THIS AGE OF ACCOUNTABILITY, IT SHOULD BE ON THE DESK OF EVERY SCHOOL PSYCHOLOGIST. The book splendidly achieves its goal—to illustrate how school psychologists can evaluate their interventions in a rigorous, scientific manner and yet do so in a way that is both feasible and practical for applied settings. Single-subject designs are ideally suited to the work of school psychologists and the topics covered in this book reflect the real-life problems confronting them. Excellently conceived and rigorously evaluated interventions are described for increasing reading and arithmetic fluency, reducing anxiety, increasing on-task behavior, and reducing transition time." (Jeff Sigafoos, PhD, Professor, Department of Special Education, The University of Texas at Austin)*

Computers in the Delivery of Special Education and Related Services: Developing Collaborative and Individualized Learning Environments, *edited by Louis J. Kruger, PsyD (Vol. 17, No. 1/2, 2002). *"An excellent compendium. . . . The topics selected cover a broad conceptual spectrum, yet provide specific and useful information for the practitioner. A valuable resource for professionals at all levels. I highly recommend it." (David G. Gotthelf, PhD, Director of Student Services, Lincoln-Sudbury Regional School District, Massachusetts)*

Inclusion Practices with Special Needs Students: Theory, Research, and Application, *edited by Steven I. Pfeiffer, PhD, ABPP, and Linda A. Reddy, PhD (Vol. 15, No. 1/2, 1999). *Provides a much needed and balanced perspective of the issues faced by educators committed to understanding how to best serve children with disabilities in schools.*

Emerging School-Based Approaches for Children with Emotional and Behavioral Problems: Research and Practice in Service Integration, *edited by Robert J. Illback, PsyD, and C. Michael Nelson, EdD (Vol. 10, No. 2, and Vol. 11, No. 1/2, 1996). *"A stimulating and valuable contribution to the topic." (Donald K. Routh, PhD, Professor of Psychology, University of Miami)*

Educational Outcomes for Students with Disabilities, *edited by James E. Ysseldyke, PhD, and Martha L. Thurlow (Vol. 9, No. 2, 1995). *"Clearly directed at teaching staff, psychologists, and other educationists but has relevance to all who work with children and young people with disabilities in schools of further education. . . . A useful book." (Physiotherapy)*

Promoting Student Success Through Group Interventions, *edited by Joseph E. Zins, EdD, and Maurice J. Elias, PhD (Vol. 8, No. 1, 1994). *"Contains clear, concise, and practical descriptions of a variety of group interventions designed to promote students' success in school and life." (Social Work with Groups Newsletter)*

Promoting Success with At-Risk Students: Emerging Perspectives and Practical Approaches, *edited by Louis J. Kruger, PsyD (Vol. 5, No. 3/4, 1990). *"Essential to professionals interested in new developments in the education of at-risk students, guidelines for implementation of approaches, and the prevention of student crises and discipline problems." (Virginia Child Protection Newsletter)*

Leadership and Supervision in Special Services: Promising Ideas and Practices, *edited by Leonard C. Burrello, EdD, and David E. Greenburg, EdD (Vol. 4, No. 1/2, 1988). *A rich source of ideas for administrative personnel involved in the delivery of special educational programs and services to children with handicapping conditions.*

School-Based Affective and Social Interventions, *edited by Susan G. Forman, PhD (Vol. 3, No. 3/4, 1988). *"Provides a valuable starting point for the psychologist, counselor, or other special service provider, special educator, regular classroom teacher, nurse, vice-principal, or other administrator who is willing to get involved in the struggle to help children and adolescents feel good about themselves and get along better in this world." (Journal of Pediatric Nursing)*

Facilitating Cognitive Development: International Perspectives, Programs, and Practices, *edited by Milton S. Schwebel and Charles A. Maher, PsyD (Vol. 3, No. 1/2, 1986). *Experts discuss the vital aspects of programs and services that will facilitate cognitive development in children and adolescents.*

Emerging Perspectives on Assessment of Exceptional Children, *edited by Randy Elliot Bennett, EdD, and Charles A. Maher, PsyD (Vol. 2, No. 2/3, 1986). *"Contains a number of innovative and promising approaches to the topic of assessment. It is an important addition to the rapidly changing field of special education and should be read by any individual who is interested in the assessment of exceptional children." (Journal of Psychological Assessment)*

Health Promotion in the Schools: Innovative Approaches to Facilitating Physical and Emotional Well-Being, *edited by Joseph E. Zins, Donald I. Wagner, and Charles A. Maher, PsyD (Vol. 1, No. 3, 1985). *"Examines new approaches to promoting physical and emotional well-being in the schools. . . . A good introduction to new-style health education." (Curriculum Review)*

Microcomputers and Exceptional Children, *edited by Randy Elliot Bennett, EdD, and Charles A. Maher, PsyD (Vol. 1, No. 1, 1984). *"This volume provides both the experienced and novice micro buff with a solid overview of the potential and real uses of the technology with exceptional students." (Alex Thomas, PhD, Port Clinton, Ohio)*

Single-Subject Designs for School Psychologists

Christopher H. Skinner, PhD
Editor

Single-Subject Designs for School Psychologists has been co-published simultaneously as *Journal of Applied School Psychology*, Volume 20, Number 2 2004.

The Haworth Press, Inc.

New York • London • Victoria (AU)
www.HaworthPress.com

Single-Subject Designs for School Psychologists has been co-published simultaneously as *Journal of Applied School Psychology*™, Volume 20, Number 2 2004.

The development, preparation, and publication of this work has been undertaken with great care. However, the publisher, employees, editors, and agents of The Haworth Press and all imprints of The Haworth Press, Inc., including The Haworth Medical Press® and Pharmaceutical Products Press®, are not responsible for any errors contained herein or for consequences that may ensue from use of materials or information contained in this work. Opinions expressed by the author(s) are not necessarily those of The Haworth Press, Inc. With regard to case studies, identities and circumstances of individuals discussed herein have been changed to protect confidentiality. Any resemblance to actual persons, living or dead, is entirely coincidental.

Cover design by Marylouise Doyle

Library of Congress Cataloging-in-Publication Data

Single-subject designs for school psychologists / Christopher H. Skinner, editor.
    p. cm.
    "Co-published simultaneously as Journal of applied school psychology, volume 20, number 2 2004."
    Includes bibliographical references and index.
    ISBN 0-7890-2825-5 (hard cover : alk. paper) – ISBN 0-7890-2826-3 (soft cover : alk. paper)
    1. School psychology. I. Skinner, Christopher H. II. Journal of applied school psychology.
LB1027.55.S57 2004
371.4–dc22
                                                          2004026211

Indexing, Abstracting & Website/Internet Coverage

This section provides you with a list of major indexing & abstracting services and other tools for bibliographic access. That is to say, each service began covering this periodical during the year noted in the right column. Most Websites which are listed below have indicated that they will either post, disseminate, compile, archive, cite or alert their own Website users with research-based content from this work. (This list is as current as the copyright date of this publication.)

(continued)

* **Exact start date to come**

(continued)

*Special Bibliographic Notes related to special journal issues
(separates) and indexing/abstracting:*

- indexing/abstracting services in this list will also cover material in any "separate" that is co-published simultaneously with Haworth's special thematic journal issue or DocuSerial. Indexing/abstracting usually covers material at the article/chapter level.
- monographic co-editions are intended for either non-subscribers or libraries which intend to purchase a second copy for their circulating collections.
- monographic co-editions are reported to all jobbers/wholesalers/approval plans. The source journal is listed as the "series" to assist the prevention of duplicate purchasing in the same manner utilized for books-in-series.
- to facilitate user/access services all indexing/abstracting services are encouraged to utilize the co-indexing entry note indicated at the bottom of the first page of each article/chapter/contribution.
- this is intended to assist a library user of any reference tool (whether print, electronic, online, or CD-ROM) to locate the monographic version if the library has purchased this version but not a subscription to the source journal.
- individual articles/chapters in any Haworth publication are also available through the Haworth Document Delivery Service (HDDS).

Single-Subject Designs
for School Psychologists

CONTENTS

ABOUT THE EDITOR

Christopher H. Skinner received his PhD in School Psychology from Lehigh University in 1989. He is Professor and Coordinator of School Psychology Programs at The University of Tennessee. His research interests include prevention and remediation of children's academic and social problems, applied experimental research, behavioral assessment, and applied behavioral analysis. He is currently serving as co-editor of *Journal of Behavioral Education.* Along with his students and colleagues, Dr. Skinner has contributed to the empirical validation of intervention process by conducting and publishing experiments using single-subject design methodologies (i.e., withdrawal designs, multiple baseline designs, alternating treatment designs, and change criterion designs) to evaluate and compare the effects of applied interventions.

Single-Subject Designs:
Procedures that Allow School Psychologists to Contribute to the Intervention Evaluation and Validation Process

Christopher H. Skinner

University of Tennessee

Like many undergraduate psychology students, I received training in traditional social science research (i.e., group-design and analysis procedures) and was required to conduct a scientific study using such procedures. I conducted an experiment in a laboratory setting where I manipulated tones and measured the effects on time perception of undergraduate students. The laboratory setting made it easy to control confounding variables, and technical equipment allowed for precise manipulation of the independent variable and measurement of the dependent variable. This experience was invaluable in that it allowed *me*, the researcher, to gain experience in the scientific process of evaluating cause-and-effect relationships. However, the same cannot be said for the undergraduate students who served as subjects for my experiment.

Address correspondence to: Christopher H. Skinner, PhD, The University of Tennessee, College of EHHS, Claxton Complex A-518, Knoxville, TN 37996-3452 (E-mail: cskinne1@utk.edu).

[Haworth co-indexing entry note]: "Single-Subject Designs: Procedures that Allow School Psychologists to Contribute to the Intervention Evaluation and Validation Process." Skinner, Christopher H. Co-published simultaneously in *Journal of Applied School Psychology* (The Haworth Press, Inc.) Vol. 20, No. 2, 2004, pp. 1-10; and: *Single-Subject Designs for School Psychologists* (ed: Christopher H. Skinner) The Haworth Press, Inc., 2004, pp. 1-10. Single or multiple copies of this article are available for a fee from The Haworth Document Delivery Service [1-800-HAWORTH, 9:00 a.m. - 5:00 p.m. (EST). E-mail address: docdelivery@haworthpress.com].

http://www.haworthpress.com/web/JAPPS
© 2004 by The Haworth Press, Inc. All rights reserved.
Digital Object Identifier: 10.1300/J008v20n02_01

While I cannot be certain, I would venture that none of my participants ever engaged in any life experiences that were enhanced because of their participation in this study. Even had I targeted a useful or functional behavior, the participants would have derived little benefit from the study as the goal was not to evaluate the effects of an intervention design to enhance their skills or ability in estimating time.

THE STUDIES IN THIS VOLUME

The articles contained in this volume include empirical case studies and experiments where researchers implemented procedures designed to control confounding variables. There are several common threads across all the studies. First, each study involved the implementation of an intervention designed to target useful or functional behaviors. Second, in all the studies, the participants' behavior improved. Thus, these studies differ from my undergraduate study in that the participants in these studies benefited from their participation. Third, each intervention was based on previous applied and theoretical research. Thus, each study demonstrated the application of the scientist-practitioner or data-based problem-solving model. In all studies, researchers used within-subject repeated measures of behavior which allowed for frequent evaluation of behavior change. Finally, all studies have both strengths and weaknesses related to drawing cause-and-effect conclusions.

In the first two studies (Campbell & Skinner, and Sharp & Skinner) school psychology students serving as consultants worked with teachers who asked for assistance. In both studies, a behavioral consultation model of service delivery was used which involved the collection of baseline and intervention phase data (Bergan, 1977; Bergan & Kratochwill, 1990). In both studies, class-wide behavior, as opposed to the behavior of individual students (single-subjects), served as the primary dependent variable. Campbell and Skinner worked with a sixth-grade teacher to reduce the amount of time the class spent transitioning from one room to another. The intervention, the Timely Transitions Game (TTG), included (a) an interdependent group-oriented reinforcement program with randomly selected criteria, (b) public posting, and (c) explicit timing. Results showed large, immediate, and sustained decreases in transition times following the implementation of the intervention. These data suggest that the presenting problem was solved.

In the second study, Sharp and Skinner worked with a teacher who was concerned that students in her class were not reading during sustained silent reading time and were not passing comprehension quizzes based on their reading. The practitioners developed an intervention by combining paired-readings with two interdependent group contingencies. In many ways this study was similar to Campbell and Skinner's study in that (a) the intervention was class-wide, (b) researchers constructed the interventions by applying previous applied and theoretical research, (c) an empirical case-study (i.e., A-B design) was used, and (d) the class-wide data suggested an immediate and sustained change in target behaviors. Although the primary dependent variable was class-wide (i.e., the number of reading comprehension quizzes passed each week by the entire class), the practitioners also collected data on each student's behavior. These results confirmed one concern with analysis of group data–practitioners may not be able to determine which students benefit from a class-wide intervention unless individual student analysis is conducted (Michael, 1974). Individual student analysis suggested that the intervention was not very effective for four of the students, indicating the need for alternative or additional intervention procedures for these students.

Although data from these consultation cases suggest that the class target behaviors improved following the implementation of the interventions, there are several problems associated with both studies that prevent one from concluding that the intervention caused these changes. In both studies, the practitioners did not collect interobserver agreement data and the treatment integrity data that was collected was suspect (i.e., either indirect or non-systematic collection of treatment integrity). Thus, the quality of both the dependent and independent variable is suspect (Gresham, Gansle, & Noell, 1993). Perhaps the most serious problem is related to the design. Both studies involved an empirical case study (A-B design), which provided only one demonstration of experimental control. Therefore, neither study allowed the practitioners to rule out other variables (i.e., threats to internal validity including history and testing–see Campbell & Stanley, 1963) which may have caused the measured changes. Campbell and Skinner intended to use a brief withdrawal phase (i.e., A-B-A-B design) which could have provided for three demonstrations of experimental control. However, the teacher declined to withdraw the intervention, as she did not want to do anything that may cause transition times to return to pre-intervention (e.g., baseline) levels.

In the third study, Rickards-Schlichting, Kehle, and Bray evaluated the effects of a self-modeling intervention on behavioral symptoms of speech anxiety in six high school students. Although they reported using an A-B-A design, because no data were collected during the intervention phase, the researchers had only pre-intervention data and post-intervention data. Thus, the strengths and weaknesses of this study may be better understood by conceptualizing it as a series of replicated, concurrent A-B designs. In this experiment, after baseline (i.e., A-phase) data were collected, all six students were exposed to the intervention for five sessions (distributed over a 3-week period). Then, one month later, follow-up (i.e., B-phase) data were collected. Results showed large changes in behavioral symptoms of speech anxiety across all students.

As similar changes in behavior were seen across all participants, researchers provided six replications of treatment effects. However, the changes occurred over the same time (over a 7-week period), with students from the same school, after each had been assessed five times. Thus, it is possible that all recorded changes may have been caused by some confounding variable(s). While the authors suggest that these changes were immediate and/or dramatic, it is important to note that the intervention phase lasted 3 weeks, and changes were measured one month after the last intervention session. Thus, there were no procedures in place to assess for immediate or dramatic change. Therefore, it is possible that threats to internal validity (i.e., history, maturation, testing) account for these changes. For example, other experiences and instruction at their school over the course of the 7-week period may have caused these changes. Although these limitations are serious threats to internal validity, this series of simultaneous A-B empirical case studies has applied value. Specifically, as the researchers' introduction reveals, previous studies had already been conducted that provided empirical evidence for the effectiveness of the self-modeling intervention. This study does provide additional evidence supporting these previous investigations. Also, because the data suggest that this procedure was effective across six additional students, the study enhances the research base related to the external validity of the self-modeling intervention.

The fourth study by Trolinder, Choi, and Proctor, differs from the previous three in that the researchers attempt to apply single-subject design procedures in order to control for threats to internal validity and more clearly establish a cause-and-effect relationship between their treatment, delayed directive praise, and increases in the on-task behavior of two children. Specifically, the researchers used a withdrawal design (i.e., A-B-A-B phases). With this design, baseline data is collected (A-phase), and then a treatment is implemented (B-phase). Comparisons across these phases allow for the first demonstration of treatment effectiveness. Next, the treatment is withdrawn and experimental conditions are returned to baseline conditions. Comparisons across the first B-phase and second A-phase (withdrawal phase) allows for the second demonstration of experimental control. Finally, provided the data from the second A-phase return to previous baseline levels, then the re-implementation of treatment allows for the third demonstration of experimental control.

A withdrawal design is powerful but has several limitations (Barlow & Hersen, 1984). First, as the Campbell and Skinner study showed, practitioners may not be willing to withdraw effective treatments. Second, when interventions alter target behaviors that are likely to be reinforced in natural environments (e.g., classrooms), those behaviors may not regress (i.e., return to baseline levels) when the intervention is withdrawn. From an applied perspective, this is positive and suggests that the intervention resulted in changes in behavior that are sustained long after the treatment is withdrawn. This may be what Rickards-Schlichting et al. found with their B-phase data which was collected one month after treatment. Regardless, when researchers employ A-B-A-B withdrawal designs and the behaviors improve during the initial treatment phase but fail to regress after the treatment is withdrawn, researchers are left with only one demonstration of experimental control (similar to Campbell & Skinner, and Sharp & Skinner). Thus, although Trolinder et al. attempted to implement an experimental design, because the data did not reverse, one cannot rule out the possibility that other confounding variables (i.e., threats to internal validity) accounted for the measured changes in behavior.

Practitioners often develop creative or novel interventions that they use to address presenting problems. However, in many instances, their data does not allow for cause-and-effect conclusions. Yet, these studies may contribute to the development and empirical validation of interventions as others can conduct follow-up studies which more clearly establish a causal relationship between the intervention and behavior change. This process is demonstrated in the Yarbrough, Skinner, Lee, and Lemmons study.

Yarbrough et al. used an intervention package similar, although not identical to, the TTG employed by Campbell and Skinner. Additionally, Yarbrough et al. used scientific procedures to evaluate the effects of the intervention (i.e., TTG) on student transition times. A multi-phase withdrawal design was used which allowed for five within-class demonstrations of experimental control. Furthermore, direct observation data were collected which suggested that both experimental procedures (treatment and withdrawal phase sessions) and data collection procedures were implemented as described. With five within-group demonstrations of experimental control, their results suggested the TTG did, in fact, cause reductions in transition times. Thus, although the Campbell and Skinner study provided poor evidence of a cause-and-effect relationship, it did have heuristic value (Malone, 1990), in that this empirical case study caused Yarbrough et al. to conduct an experiment on the TTG which provided much more valid evidence that the TTG caused decreases in transition times.

The next two studies are both variations of the multiple-baseline design. The first study by Winn, Skinner, Allin, and Hawkins is actually three separate behavioral consultation cases. However, because the practitioners (teachers and consultants) employed similar intervention strategies and dependent variables, these cases could be combined. Additionally, by coincidence, the practitioners used a different number of baseline sessions across each case. Thus, the three non-concurrent cases could be combined to form a non-concurrent, multiple-baseline, across-subjects design (Watson & Workman, 1981). This design provided for three replications of experimental control, across three subjects, in three different classrooms, at three different times. As this design controlled for most threats to internal validity, the results support the conclusion that the self-managed intervention strategy did cause the changes in student writing behavior.

The final study, by McCallum, Skinner, and Hutchins provides the only example of single-subject design research in this volume that included only one subject. In this study, researchers used a multiple-probe design to evaluate the effects of the tape-problems intervention on student mathematics fact fluency. The multiple-probe design is similar to a multiple-baseline design, except that assessment-only baseline sessions are not run as frequently. This is done to minimize testing effects, including the possibility that the students become frustrated by constantly being assessed on tasks that are not being targeted with the intervention (Cuvo, 1979). In the McCallum et al. study, staggered (as opposed to concurrent, see Rickards-Schlichting et al.) replications were performed across tasks (as opposed to across subjects, see Winn et al.). Staggering the treatment across sets of problems (tasks) served both an experimental and applied purpose. From an experimental perspective, staggering the intervention across sets of items allowed for three non-concurrent, within-subjects demonstrations of experimental control (Hayes, 1985). These procedures control for several confounding variables, including testing and history effects. From an applied perspective, it would have been overwhelming to target over 60 different facts simultaneously. Thus, targeting only 21 or 22 facts at a time likely increased the probability of the intervention being effective and the student experiencing success.

SUMMARY

None of the researchers who conducted the first three studies in this volume (Campbell & Skinner; Rickards-Schlichting et al.; Sharp & Skinner) used traditional experimental design procedures to control for threats to internal validity. Although Trolinder et al. attempted to use design elements (e.g., treatment withdrawal) to establish experimental control, this strategy was unsuccessful. Thus, none of the first four studies allow us to rule out a plethora of confounding variables that may have caused the change in behavior. This prevents us from concluding that the intervention caused desired behavior change. However, in each of the first four studies, the participants' lives appeared to be improved. Room-to-room transitions were made more efficient, allowing more time for teaching and learning (Campbell & Skinner). Students began reading during sustained silent-reading time and passed more comprehension tests (Sharp & Skinner). Such behaviors are likely to enhance reading skills. High school students improved their public speaking skills and reported feeling more confident and less anxious when speaking in public (Rickards-Schlichting et al.). Finally, two students who often failed to sustain their attention were now engaging in high rates of on-task behavior (Trolinder et al.). Such behaviors can enhance learning and decrease inappropriate behaviors across settings and tasks (Lentz, 1988). Thus, despite limitations in establishing cause-and-effect relationships, the evidence collected suggests that the participants in these studies were all better off for having participated.

Additionally, the four studies which failed to control for threats to internal validity do have value. The heuristic value of the Campbell and Skinner study is confirmed by the Yarbrough et al. study. Currently, researchers are conducting an additional study designed to empirically validate the results of the Sharp and Skinner study. The Trolinder et al. study suggests that delayed praise may enhance maintenance of behavior change, perhaps more than immediate praise. This provides a clear direction for future research that has important applied implications. Finally, the Rickards-Schlichting et al. study provided additional evidence of the effectiveness of the self-modeling interventions, thus enhancing the external validity of the intervention.

In the subsequent three studies, experimenters successfully employed single-subject design strategies to control for threats to internal validity. Thus, these three studies increase our confidence in concluding that the intervention caused the measured changes in behavior. However, in each of these cases, the interventions were comprised on multiple components. These components were not chosen or developed out of thin air or based on intuition. Rather, previous applied and theoretical science suggested that each component could bring about the desired change in behavior. Thus, although these more tightly controlled applied studies allow us more confidence in concluding that the intervention caused the desired effects, they do not allow us to determine which component or combination of components (interaction effects) caused the change. Therefore, from an applied perspective, these studies empirically validated the interventions, but provide very imprecise data with respect to specific cause-and-effect relationships between intervention components and behavior change. Thus, these studies may do little to enhance the theoretical research base that demands more precise understanding of cause-and-effect relationships (Hughes, 2000). However, as with the other four studies, each provides clear directions for future theoretical research.

While school psychologists are encouraged to use empirically validated interventions and contribute to this research base (Kratochwill & Stoiber, 2002; Stoiber & Kratochwill, 2000), school psychology literature contains few examples of intervention research (Robinson, Skinner, & Brown, 1998). Perhaps one cause of this dearth of intervention research is an under-emphasis on training and applying single-subject design procedures. School psychologists often receive referral to address *individual* student problems or *class-wide* problems. As school psychologists attempt to remedy presenting problems, single-subject design research methodologies may allow them to frequently evaluate the students' progress (e.g., behavior change over time). These frequent evaluations can provide evidence of intervention effectiveness and allow practitioners to make decisions such as whether to continue, alter, or cease intervention procedures. By making slight alterations in their evaluation procedures to include single-subject design methods, school psychologists may be able to simultaneously conduct experiments that control for threats to internal validity and thereby contribute to the process of developing and empirically validating interventions.

As a field, school psychologists have promoted and discussed empirically-validated, empirically-supported, and evidence-based interventions. We have talked enough. It is time for school psychologists to *get to the doing* and begin developing interventions and conducting and disseminating intervention research. Perhaps this special collection will encourage researchers, practitioners, and trainers of school psychologists to consider using single-subject design research procedures to help us build the research base we require to effectively remedy presenting problems.

REFERENCES

Barlow, D. H., & Hersen, M. (1984). *Single case experimental designs: Strategies for studying behavior change, 2nd Ed.* New York: Pergamon.

Bergan, J. R. (1977). *Behavioral Consultation.* New York: Charles E Merrill.

Bergan, J. R., & Kratochwill, T. R. (1990). *Behavioral consultation and therapy.* New York: Plenum Press.

Campbell, S., & Skinner, C. H. (2004). Combining explicit timing with an interdependent group contingency program to decrease transitions times: An investigation of the Timely Transitions Game. *Journal of Applied School Psychology, 20*(2), 11-27.

Campbell, D. T., & Stanley, J. C. (1963). *Experimental and quasi-experimental designs for research.* Skokie, IL: Rand McNally.

Cuvo, A. J. (1979). Multiple-baseline design in instructional research: Pitfalls of measurement and procedural advantages. *American Journal of Mental Deficiency, 84,* 219-228.

Gresham, F. M., Gansle, K. A., & Noell, G. H. (1993). Treatment integrity in applied behavior analysis with children. *Journal of Applied Behavior Analysis, 26,* 257-263.

Hayes, S. C. (1985). Natural multiple baseline across persons: A reply to Harris and Jenson. *Behavioral Assessment, 7,* 129-132.

Hughes, J. N. (2000). Reconsideration of the role of theory in psychosocial intervention. *Journal of School Psychology, 38,* 389-401.

Kratochwill, T. R., & Stoiber, K. C. (2002). Evidence-based interventions in school psychology: Conceptual foundations of the *Procedural and Coding Manual of Division 16 and the Society for the Study of School Psychology Task Force. School Psychology Quarterly, 17,* 341-389.

Lentz, F. E. (1988). On-task behavior, academic performance, and classroom disruptions: Untangling the target selection problem in classroom interventions. *School Psychology Review, 17,* 243-257.

Malone, J. C. (1990). *Theories of learning: A historical approach.* Belmont, CA: Wadsworth.

McCallum, E., Skinner, C. H., & Hutchins, H. (2004). The taped-problems intervention: Increasing division fact fluency using a low-tech self-managed time-delay intervention. *Journal of Applied School Psychology, 20*(2), 129-147.

Michael, J. (1974). Statistical inference for individual organism research: Mixed blessing or curse? *Journal of Applied Behavior Analysis, 7,* 647-653.

Rickards-Schlichting, K. A., Kehle, T. J., & Bray, M. A. (2004). A self-modeling intervention for high school students with public speaking anxiety. *Journal of Applied School Psychology, 20*(2), 47-60.

Robinson, S. L., Skinner, C. H., & Brown, C. S. (1998). An analysis of articles appearing in school psychology journals from 1985-1994. *Proven practices: Prevention and Remediation Solutions for Schools, 1,* 28-33.

Sharp, S. R., & Skinner, C. H. (2004). Using interdependent group contingencies with randomly selected criteria and paired reading to enhance class-wide reading performance. *Journal of Applied School Psychology, 20*(2), 29-45.

Stoiber, K. C., & Kratochwill, T. R. (2000). Empirically supported interventions and school psychology: Rationale and methodological issues-Part I. *School Psychology Quarterly, 15,* 75-105.

Trolinder, D. M., Choi, H., & Proctor, T. B. (2004). Use of delayed praise as a directive and its effectiveness on on-task behavior. *Journal of Applied School Psychology, 20*(2), 61-83.

Watson, P. J., & Workman, E. A. (1981). The non-concurrent multiple baseline across-individuals design: An extension of the traditional multiple baseline design. *Journal of Behavior Therapy and Experimental Psychiatry, 12,* 257-259.

Winn, B. D., Skinner, C. H., Allin, J. D., & Hawkins, J. A. (2004). Practicing school consultants can empirically validate interventions: A description and demonstration of the non-concurrent multiple-baseline design. *Journal of Applied School Psychology, 20*(2), 109-128.

Yarbrough, J. L., Skinner, C. H., Lee. Y. J., & Lemmons, C. (2004). Decreasing transition times in a second grade classroom: Scientific support for the Timely Transitions Game. *Journal of Applied School Psychology, 20*(2), 85-108.

Combining Explicit Timing with an Interdependent Group Contingency Program to Decrease Transition Times: An Investigation of the Timely Transitions Game

Stephanie Campbell

Southpointe Family Resource Center, P. C.

Christopher H. Skinner

University of Tennessee

SUMMARY. A sixth-grade teacher and consultant serving as a behavioral specialist developed, implemented, and evaluated the Timely Transitions Game (TTG), a procedure designed to reduce room-to-room transition times. The TTG combined several procedures that have been shown to alter student behavior including explicit timing procedures and an interdependent, group-oriented reward program with randomly se-

Address correspondence to: Christopher H. Skinner, PhD, The University of Tennessee, College of EHHS, Claxton Complex A-518, Knoxville, TN 37996-3452 (E-mail: cskinne1@utk.edu).

[Haworth co-indexing entry note]: "Combining Explicit Timing with an Interdependent Group Contingency Program to Decrease Transition Times: An Investigation of the Timely Transitions Game." Campbell, Stephanie, and Christopher H. Skinner. Co-published simultaneously in *Journal of Applied School Psychology* (The Haworth Press, Inc.) Vol. 20, No. 2, 2004, pp. 11-27; and: *Single-Subject Designs for School Psychologists* (ed: Christopher H. Skinner) The Haworth Press, Inc., 2004, pp. 11-27. Single or multiple copies of this article are available for a fee from The Haworth Document Delivery Service [1-800-HAWORTH, 9:00 a.m. - 5:00 p.m. (EST). E-mail address: docdelivery@haworthpress.com].

lected criteria. Five transition times were measured and recorded each day. At the end of the school day, the teacher randomly selected a transition and a criterion (seconds taken to transition). If the class completed the randomly selected transition in less time than the randomly selected criterion, they earned a letter. When students earned enough letters (e.g., the five letters that spell *M-U-S-I-C*), they received access to the reward (e.g., listening to music during independent seat-work). Results indicated immediate and sustained decreases in transition times following the implementation of the intervention. Although methodological concerns prevent drawing cause-and-effect conclusions, the current study shows how educators can adapt and combine empirically validated strategies and procedures to remedy presenting problems. *[Article copies available for a fee from The Haworth Document Delivery Service: 1-800-HAWORTH. E-mail address: <docdelivery@haworthpress.com> Website: <http://www. HaworthPress.com> © 2004 by The Haworth Press, Inc. All rights reserved.]*

KEYWORDS. Empirical case study, behavioral consultation, class-wide interventions, unknown criteria, Timely Transitions Game

Researchers investigating opportunities to respond have found that increasing the number of accurate, active, academic responses enhances learning (e.g., Greenwood, Delquadri, & Hall, 1984). Two general strategies for increasing opportunities to respond include increasing student response rates and making more time available for learning (Gettinger, 1995; Skinner, Belfiore, Mace, Williams, & Johns, 1997). Making more time available by adding days to the school year (e.g., increase school days per year from 180 to 220) or increasing years in school (e.g., pre-school and graduate school) can enhance learning but are expensive strategies that reduce time available for other behaviors (Skinner, Belfiore, & Watson, 1995/2002). Other strategies increase time available for learning activities by reducing time spent engaged in non-academic activities, such as time spent transitioning from one room to another (Paine, 1983).

Room-to-room transitions are required, but take time, which may be lengthened when students engage in inappropriate behaviors. During room-to-room transitions, students may be more likely to engage in inappropriate behaviors because (a) teachers have more difficulty monitoring student behaviors during transitions, (b) students are in closer physical proximity to each other, and/or (c) there are few competing behavior options that may be reinforced (Myerson & Hale, 1984; Skinner, Wallace, & Neddenriep, 2002).

Often, educators respond to inappropriate transition behavior with punishment procedures. When teachers can identify specific students who engage in inappropriate behavior, only those students receive the aversive consequence or punishment. In other instances, educators cannot identify who engaged in inappropriate transition behavior. In these situations, educators may spend additional time investigating incidents (e.g., to determine who engaged in what behavior first) or they may punish the entire group (Henington & Skinner, 1998; Skinner, Neddenriep, Robinson, Ervin, & Jones, 2002). Sometimes punishment involves lengthening transition times. For example, teachers may make the entire class wait quietly in the hall until everyone is quiet. While such punishment procedures may help reduce future inappropriate behaviors, they often increase transition times, further reducing time available for learning (Paine, 1983).

One antecedent procedure that may help decrease transition times is explicit or overt timing. During overt timing, students are given instructions and a stopwatch is started in plain view of the students. Overt timing has been shown to enhance students' speed of academic responding (e.g., Derr & Shapiro, 1989; Derr-Minneci & Shapiro, 1992; Rhymer, Skinner, Henington, D'Reaux, & Sims, 1998; Rhymer, Skinner, Jackson, McNeill, Smith, & Jackson, 2002; Van Houten & Thompson, 1976). However, researchers and educators have not explored the use of explicit timing as a strategy for remedying class-wide behavior problems, such as reducing room-to-room transition times.

Overt or explicit timing procedures may be effective because students have a history of being reinforced for rapid responding when their behavior is being timed (Van Houten & Thompson, 1976). If this causal hypothesis is accurate, then failure to reinforce rapid responding after the implementation of overt timing may cause extinction. Thus, maintaining the effects of overt timing may require additional reinforcement for more rapid responding.

Group contingencies may be the most appropriate mechanism for reinforcing more rapid transitions (Page & Edwards, 1978; Skinner, Cashwell, & Skinner, 2000; Stage & Quiroz, 1997; Upson & Skinner, 2002). There are three types of group contingencies: independent, interdependent, and dependent (Litow & Pumroy, 1975). With independent group contingencies, only students whose behavior meets a criterion receive access to consequences. With dependent group contingencies, the entire class receives access to consequences contingent upon one student's behavior. With interdependent group contingencies, everyone receives access to consequences contingent upon some group criteria (e.g., class average).

With independent or dependent group contingencies, criteria are based on individual student behavior. These contingencies may be inappropriate for reducing typical classroom-to-classroom transition times. When moving from class-to-class, students move as a group, often in single file, and one student is not permitted to transition any faster than the entire group. Thus, the target behavior (i.e., time to transition) incorporates across-classmate interdependencies, as each student's rate of transition is dependent upon her/his classmates' transition behavior. Interdependent group contingencies may best address room-to-room transitions because the contingency also incorporates interdependencies as all or none of the students receive access to reinforcement based on the *group meeting* a *group-oriented* criterion (Lew, Mesch, Johnson, & Johnson, 1986).

There are practical advantages associated with interdependent group contingencies. Because all-or-none of the students receive access to reinforcement, these contingencies may reduce reinforcement stealing, reinforcer belittling, and social side effects associated with some students not earning reinforcers (Skinner, Cashwell, & Dunn, 1996). It is easy to deliver tangible reinforcers to everyone, as opposed to delivering reinforcers only to students who earned them (Axelrod, 1973; Gresham & Gresham, 1982; Lew et al., 1986; Turco & Elliott, 1990). Additionally, delivering reinforcers to all-or-none of the students allows educators to use resource-efficient activity reinforcers (Skinner et al., 1996). Finally, interdependent group reinforcement programs may encourage classmates to cooperate and help one another succeed in order to increase the probability of the group earning their reinforcement (Slavin, 1987).

While interdependent group reinforcement programs can be effective, there are limitations associated with such programs. One limitation is associated with the criteria. With individual contingencies (e.g., a behavioral contract), when a student judges that they can no longer meet a criterion for earning reinforcement, they may become frustrated, give up, and/or misbehave. Similar reactions may occur across all students if the entire class begins to lose confidence in their ability to earn a reward. Skinner et al. (1996) suggested that randomly selecting criteria and/or target behaviors might reduce this negative side effect. However, only three studies using interdependent group contingencies with randomly selected criteria and/or target behaviors have been conducted.

These studies showed that these procedures were effective in reducing disruptive behavior (Kelshaw-Levering, Sterling-Turner, Henry, & Skinner, 2000; Theodore, Bray, Kehle, & Jenson, 2001) and enhancing academic performance (Popkin & Skinner, 2003).

School psychologists are encouraged to address presenting problems via the application of empirically validated, supported, or evidence-based theories, strategies, and/or procedures (Hughes, 2000; Kratochwill & Stoiber, 2002; Stoiber & Kratochwill, 2000). The purpose of the current manuscript is to describe an empirical case study in which a teacher and a behavior specialist developed, implemented, and evaluated an intervention that combined explicit timing and interdependent group contingencies to reduce transition times in a sixth-grade general education classroom.

METHOD

Participants and Setting

Participants included 30 sixth-grade students (26 African-American students and four Caucasian students) in a rural Southeastern public school. The teacher was a Caucasian woman with 12 years teaching experience. She requested assistance from a behavior specialist to address problems with transitions. The teacher indicated that her students often engaged in inappropriate behaviors during transitions (e.g., talking, touching each other, failure to follow directions) and that the time required to address these behaviors was increasing transition times and reducing time available for academic activities. The behavior specialist was working half-time for the district and was in her final year of a Ph.D. program in school psychology.

The classroom contained 30 student desks, arranged in five columns with six rows, facing a blackboard and the teacher's desk. As students entered the room, student desks were immediately to the left, blackboard to the right, and the teacher's desk was straight ahead on the other side of the room. Between the front row of the desks and the blackboard was approximately 7 feet of empty space that was used as the area to "line up" prior to transitions from the room.

Materials

A digital stopwatch was used to measure transition times. Two plastic containers were used to store pieces of paper with transitions or criteria printed on them. The transitions container had five slips of folded paper with one of the following five transitions printed on each slip of paper: "going to recess," "back from recess," "going to lunch," "back from lunch," or "going to specials." The teacher was not concerned with transition times returning from "specials" (e.g., music class, art class) because there were only 20 minutes left in the school day and academic activities were less structured.

Other materials included teacher-purchased or rented reinforcers (e.g., popcorn, movie) and a chart constructed by the behavior specialist. The chart was drawn on yellow-poster board and included eight columns. Figure 1 depicts an example of the chart. In the first column was space to record the date. In columns two through six were spaces to record the number of seconds taken going to recess, returning from recess, going to lunch, returning from lunch, and going to "specials," respectively. In the seventh column was space for recording the criterion time that was drawn from the container at the end of the day. The teacher indicated which transition was drawn from the jar by putting a star next to the time for that transition on the day. When a criterion was met, a letter was recorded in the last column. If the criterion was not met, a dash was recorded in the last column.

Procedures

Design and Baseline Phase. A withdrawal design (A-B-A-B) was planned. However, after the intervention was put in place, the teacher declined to implement even a brief withdrawal of the treatment. Therefore, an empirical case study, consisting of a baseline, or A-phase, and an intervention, or B-phase, was used to evaluate the effects of the intervention. Throughout baseline, the teacher used her typical procedures to

FIGURE 1. Example of the TTG Feedback Chart Where T-1 Through T-5 Represent the Five Daily Transitions (Going to Recess, Returning from Recess, Going to Lunch, Returning from Lunch, and Going to "Specials," Respectively) and * Indicates the Transition That Was Selected for That Day.

Date	To Recess	From Recess	To Lunch	From Lunch	To Specials	Randomly Selected Time	P-A-R-T-Y
11/7	379	122*	57	66	172	132	P
11/8	221*	52	64	92	60	50	-
11/9	89	79	101	71	74*	122	A

transition students. The consultant (i.e., the behavior specialist) covertly used a stopwatch to measure the time that elapsed between the teacher indicating it was time to line up and the teacher allowing the students to file out of the classroom. This generally included informing the students that it was time to line up, waiting for students to be quiet and seated at their desks, prompting silence and in-seat behavior for certain students, then releasing students one row at a time into a line facing the door between the first row of desks and the blackboard. Typically, after students were in line, the teacher would wait for the students to behave appropriately (e.g., quiet, facing forward, with hands to self) before allowing them to leave the classroom. After the students were instructed to leave the room, the consultant stopped timing the students. During transitions when students misbehaved, the teacher stopped the class and started the stopwatch. When the students engaged in appropriate line behavior, she stopped the stopwatch and instructed the students to continue transitioning. The transition was over when the last student crossed the threshold of the destination room.

Teaching the Intervention. After baseline data had been collected, the consultant reviewed appropriate transition behaviors and introduced the explicit timing procedure to the students. The consultant then described and demonstrated behaviors that indicated the students were ready to line up (e.g., desk cleared, sitting in one's seat quietly). Upon prompting, all class members demonstrated *ready to line up behavior*. Then appropriate line behavior (i.e., standing between the student ahead and behind oneself, facing the back of the student ahead of oneself with hands and feet to self, and being silent) was described and modeled by the consultant. After prompting, the entire class exhibited *appropriate line behavior*.

Next, the Timely Transitions Game (TTG) was explained to the students. First, the explicit timing procedures were taught to the class. After delivering the prompt: *"it is time to line up now,"* the teacher started the stopwatch. After all rows were exhibiting *ready to line up behavior*, the teacher dismissed rows. After the class exhibited *appropriate line behavior*, the teacher stopped the watch and allowed the students to file out of the classroom. If inappropriate line behavior occurred (e.g., talking, moving from between the student ahead and behind oneself, or touching others) while transitioning to the next room, the teacher instructed the line to stop and resumed timing (i.e., started the stopwatch until appropriate line behavior was restored). The explicit timing procedure was practiced in mock transitions to and from the music room. Students were told after each transition what their transition time was and it was recorded on the chart.

Following the explicit timing practice, the group contingency procedures were explained. Students were shown the *transitions* and *criteria* containers that remained on the teacher's desk. An example of the chart was written on the blackboard. The behavior specialist explained how the contingency would work. Each day, the date and each transition time would be recorded in the designated column. At the end of that school day, a transition would be drawn from the container and would indicate which transition time would be used to determine whether the group met the criterion for earning a reward. Next, the criterion time would be randomly selected from the other container and compared with the students' actual transition time for the randomly selected transition. When the students' transition time was less than the time drawn, the reward would be earned for the day. The immediate reward would be a letter (e.g., *P*) used to spell a word, such as *P-A-R-T-Y*. The letters earned would be recorded on the chart, which was posted for public viewing in the classroom by the door. After the word was spelled, all members of the class would receive access to the reward. On days that the class did not meet the criterion, a letter would not be earned and the teacher would write a dash on the chart. The students were told that no additional punitive actions would be taken (e.g., taking away a letter) when they did not meet the randomly selected criterion. The criteria from the criteria pool were listed on the blackboard. After a brief question and answer session, the students appeared to understand that they would not know what transition would be targeted and what time would be needed to earn reinforcement until the end of the day.

TTG Implementation. The morning following training, the behavior specialist posted the yellow feedback chart, and the teacher reminded the students of the game. The teacher informed the students that they would earn a popcorn party when they spelled out the word *P-A-R-T-Y.* When students transitioned to a room, the teacher used the stopwatch to collect explicit timing data. When they returned from the room, the teacher announced the number of seconds used to go to the room and return from the room and recorded those times on the chart. At the end of the day (final 20 minutes that occurred after specials), the teacher randomly selected a slip of paper indicating the transition and placed a star beside the time. Next, she randomly selected a criterion time and recorded it in the seventh column. If the time for that transition was less than the selected criteria, she recorded a letter (i.e., *P*). If the randomly selected transition's time was greater than the selected criteria, a dash was recorded on the chart.

An example of this procedure can be clearly understood by referring back to Figure 1. On 11/7, immediately after each transition was completed, the teacher recorded each of the transition times on the TTG chart. These times ranged from 379 seconds (going to recess) to 57 seconds (going to lunch). At the end of the day she randomly selected a transition and marked that transition time with a star (an asterisk on Figure 1). She then randomly selected a criterion (in Figure 1, 132 seconds). Thus, on 11/7, the students, randomly selected transition was less than the randomly selected criteria and the students earned their reinforcer. Thus, the teacher wrote the letter *P* on the final column. To understand the advantages of random selection refer to our example in Figure 1 which shows that on 11/7 the students had a poor initial transition when they went to recess (i.e., 379 seconds). Although this transition time exceeded all the criterion in the criteria pool, this did not mean the class had lost their opportunity to earn reinforcement that day as any of the subsequent transitions could be randomly selected at the end of the day and that randomly selected transition time would be used to determine if they met the randomly selected criterion.

Figure 1 provides an example of the students not meeting the criteria. On 11/8, the randomly selected transition time was going to recess, which was 221 seconds. The randomly selected criterion was 50 seconds. Thus, the students did not earn the reinforcer and a dash, as opposed to the letter A, was placed in the final column. In this example, because of a poor initial transition, the students did not earn their reinforcer. However, because transition times and criteria were randomly selected, the students did not know this. Thus, their subsequent transitions were still under control of the contingency. Therefore, there was still an incentive to transition well even after an initial poor transition.

Figure 1 is merely provided as an example of the procedures. These procedure were carried out throughout the intervention with reinforcers varying after each reward was earned. For example, after the students earned the popcorn party, they earned listening to music during independent seatwork *M-U-S-I-C*, going outside for lunch *P-I-C-N-I-C*, and watching a brief video *M-O-V-I-E*.

Treatment Integrity

Columns 2-6 on the chart provide evidence that the teacher implemented explicit timing; however, the extent to which this was done correctly was not gauged. The chart also indicated which transition was drawn each day (the star that was recorded next to the transition time) and the criteria time that was randomly selected. Approximately every other school day, the behavior specialist checked the chart and recorded the presence or absence of each of these seven pieces of recorded data from the day before (i.e., five transition times, a star indicating randomly selected transitions, and the number of seconds of the randomly selected criterion). Treatment integrity was calculated by dividing the number of occurrences by 7 and multiplying by 100.

RESULTS

Figure 2 displays the daily mean transition times across baseline and intervention phases. Figure 2 shows that immediately following the implementation of the intervention, students showed a substantial decline in the average amount of time taken for daily transitions. Briefer transition times were maintained throughout the course of the study. During baseline, average transitions were 278 seconds, or 4.6 minutes. With five transitions per day, approximately 23 minutes per day were spent waiting for appropriate behavior in order to transition. Over a 5-day school week, this time spent waiting was almost 2 hours (115.7 minutes). During the intervention phase, transitions averaged 69.5 seconds, or almost 29 minutes per week. Thus, average weekly transition times were reduced by approximately 1.5 hours per week following the implementation of the intervention. Effect size, calculated by dividing mean differences by the standard deviation in baseline (22.4 seconds), was large, $ES = 9.3$.

Figure 3 shows the percent of treatment integrity for each day. Treatment integrity for the first week of implementation was 100%, but decreased from weeks two through nine to approximately 75%. Despite the decrease in treatment integrity, notable treatment gains were maintained.

DISCUSSION

Effective and efficient management of room-to-room transitions allows more time for educators to teach and students to learn. The current empirical case study suggests that the teacher was able to save approximately 1.5 hours per week of allocated school time by implementing the

FIGURE 2. Daily Average Time for Transitions Across Baseline and Intervention Phases.

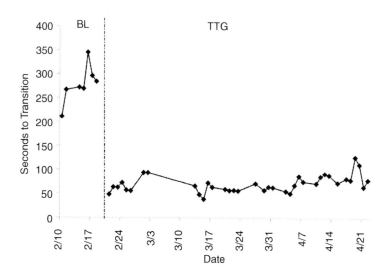

FIGURE 3. Daily Percentage of Steps Recorded on the Chart During the Intervention Phase.

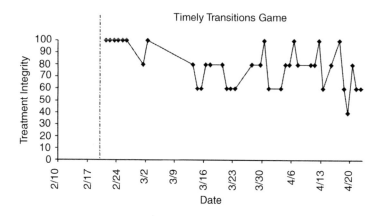

TTG, an intervention that combined explicit timing and an interdependent group contingency. While these data suggest the intervention was effective, future researchers should address several limitations associated with the current study before applied recommendations can be made.

Limitations and Future Research

In the current study, the teacher declined the option of withdrawing the program for a brief period of time. Thus, although the current study contains a control condition (i.e., the baseline phase) and an intervention condition (i.e., the treatment phase), the A-B design does not control for threats to internal validity. Therefore, a variety of confounding variables may have accounted for the abrupt reduction in transition times after the intervention was implemented. Perhaps the most serious concerns in the current study are history and instrumentation.

In the current empirical case study, another event may have occurred at approximately the same time that the intervention was implemented and resulted in the abrupt reductions in transition times. Campbell and Stanley (1966) refer to this threat to internal validity as *history*. In the current study, during the class's final room-to-room transition on the last baseline day, an event may have occurred that caused the reduction in transition times. For example, during this transition, the students may have observed another class transitioning in the hallway and the school principal was yelling at two students for misbehaving during the transition and informed them that they would receive a harsh punishment (e.g., after school suspension for a week). This event could have caused the participating group of students to behave much differently during their subsequent transitions.

In the current empirical case study, the teacher may have altered her timing procedures after the intervention was implemented. Campbell and Stanley (1966) refer to this threat to internal validity as *instrumentation*. In the current study, the teacher helped develop the intervention and the consultant informed the teacher of the previous research supporting the effectiveness of various intervention components (e.g., explicit timing, group rewards). Thus, the teacher may have had expectations that the intervention would be effective. These expectations may have caused her to alter her timing procedures during the intervention phase. Specifically, she may have become more lenient with respect to stopping and starting the stopwatch when students misbehaved during the intervention phase transitions.

To address these threats to internal validity, future researchers should conduct experimental studies using more robust designs to more clearly establish a cause-and-effect relationship. Examples of within-group designs that control for these threats to internal validity include withdrawal designs, multiple baseline designs, and alternating treatment designs (Hersen & Barlow, 1982). Additionally, to increase confidence that data collection procedures were not systematically altered, future researchers should have an independent observer simultaneously collect data and calculate interobserver agreement.

In the current study, treatment integrity data was collected using permanent product data. Specifically, every other day the behavior specialist looked at the data on the publicly posted chart. If data was written on this chart, it was assumed that the teacher performed the steps accurately. However, this assumption may not be valid. For example, just because the teacher wrote down a transition time, does not mean that she actually timed the transition accurately. Therefore, future researchers should use an independent observer to collect treatment integrity data to ensure that procedures are implemented as planned.

Assume that in the current study (a) an experimental design was used, (b) data were collected to ensure the independent variable was implemented with integrity, and (c) data were collected to ensure that the dependent variable was measured consistently. Future research on the TTG would still be needed to establish internal and external validity. The TTG consisted of several different procedures that have been shown to change students' behavior. Thus, it is not clear what role the explicit timing procedure or the group contingency played in altering the students' behavior. Previous research suggests that providing publicly posted feedback also may have contributed to the effectiveness of this intervention (Van Houten, Hill, & Parsons, 1975). Furthermore, merely instructing the students in appropriate transition behavior may have accounted for some of the effects. Thus, future researchers should conduct component analysis studies to determine which component(s) of the TTG are responsible for the effectiveness of the intervention.

Future researchers should address external validity limitations associated with the current study by conducting similar studies across other populations (e.g., grade levels, students with disabilities). In the current study, the teacher reported a notable decrease in both the intensity and frequency of inappropriate transition behaviors following the implementation of the TTG. Future researchers should use direct observation procedures to collect data on inappropriate transition behaviors to determine whether the TTG decreases these behaviors.

In the current study, the consultant asked the teacher whether she wanted to withdraw the program for a brief period of time in order to more carefully evaluate the effects of the intervention. The teacher declined. While this provides strong evidence that the teacher found the TTG acceptable and efficacious, future researchers should more formally assess both teacher and student perceptions of the intervention as such data may allow researchers to improve the intervention and make it more acceptable to other professionals and students.

CONCLUSION

The empirical data that were collected and the teacher's reports suggest that the referral problem was solved. The immediate, large, and sustained reductions in transition times after the intervention was implemented suggest that this intervention caused the reduction. However, the experimental limitations of the current empirical case study are serious and prevent us from concluding that the interventions caused the behavior changes.

Despite experimental limitations, there are several arguments suggesting that the current empirical case study warrants dissemination. First, the current study illustrated how a teacher and behavior specialist could adapt and combine empirically validated theories, strategies, and procedures to remedy presenting classroom problems. Encouraging educators to use scientific data-bases to address problems is consistent with professional practice, in general, and more specifically, with school psychology practices (Kratochwill & Stoiber, 2002; Stoiber & Kratochwill, 2000).

There are various descriptions of how science and practice interact that are incorporated into constructs such as scientist-practitioner, practitioner-scientist, data-based decision-making, and empirically-validated, empirically-supported, and evidence-based interventions. While there are subtle differences between various constructs, all include practice informing science as well as science informing practice. The second reason why the current study warrants dissemination is that it may have heuristic value. Specifically, this empirical case study may encourage future investigators to conduct scientific studies of the TTG. Such studies could (a) provide empirical validation of the TTG that more clearly establishes a cause-and-effect relationship between the intervention and reductions in transition time,[1] (b) influence other applied research, and (c) provide evidence related to the theories and assumptions that are reflected in each of the various intervention components (Hughes, 2000).

Romeo (1998) adamantly rejected the use of group contingencies to address behavior problems. Romeo appears to equate group contingencies with group punishment. Therefore, Romeo's concerns and judgments may be based on faulty assumptions and lack of information. Regardless, Romeo's (1998) article provides another justification for disseminating the current study as the results appear to refute the contention that group contingencies should never be used to address behavior problems. Specifically, the teacher's refusal to withdraw the intervention for a brief period of time supports previous researchers who found that interdependent group contingency programs are effective (Stage & Quiroz, 1997), efficient (Gresham & Gresham, 1982) and acceptable (Turco & Elliott, 1990). Thus, the current study provides evidence for the applied value of such procedures, and therefore may prevent practitioners from "throwing the baby out with the bathwater." Additionally, the current study demonstrates how creative educators can address problems by using interdependent group contingencies to reinforce alternative desired behaviors as opposed to punishing inappropriate behaviors, an application of interdependent group-oriented contingencies that seems to have been ignored by some authors.

NOTE

1. The manuscript by Yarbrough, Skinner, and Lee demonstrates that this empirical case study had heuristic value as it resulted in this scientific study that provided empirical validation of the TTG.

REFERENCES

Axelrod, S. (1973). Comparison of individual and group contingencies in two special classes. *Behavior Therapy, 4*, 83-90.
Campbell, D. T., & Stanley, J. C. (1966). *Experimental and quasi-experimental designs for research.* Boston: Houghton Mifflin Company.
Derr, T. F., & Shapiro, E. S. (1989). A behavioral evaluation of curriculum-based assessment of reading. *Journal of Psychoeducational Assessment, 7*, 148-160.
Derr-Minneci, T. F., & Shapiro, E. S. (1992). Validating curriculum-based measurement in reading from a behavioral perspective. *School Psychology Quarterly, 7*, 2-16.
Gettinger, M. (1995). Best practice of increasing academic learning time. In A. Thomas & J. Grimes (Eds.), *Best practice in school psychology-III* (pp. 945-954). Washington, DC: The National Association of School Psychologists.
Greenwood, C. R., Delquadri, J. C., & Hall, R. V. (1984). Opportunity to respond and student academic performance. In W. L. Heward, T. E. Heron, J. Trap-Porter, & D.

S. Hill (Eds.), *Focus on behavior analysis in education* (pp. 58-88). Columbus, OH: Charles Merrill.

Gresham, F. M., & Gresham, G. N. (1982). Interdependent, dependent, and independent group contingencies for controlling disruptive behavior. *Journal of Special Education, 16*, 101-110.

Henington, C., & Skinner, C. H. (1998). Peer monitoring. In K. Toppins & S. Ely (Eds.) *Peer Assisted Learning* (pp. 237-253). Hillsdale, NJ: Erlbaum.

Hersen, M., & Barlow, D. H. (1982). *Single case experimental designs: Strategies for studying behavior change.* New York: Pergamon Press.

Hughes, J. N. (2000). Reconsidering the role of theory in psychosocial intervention. *Journal of School Psychology, 38*, 389-401.

Kelshaw-Levering, K., Sterling-Turner, H. E., Henry, J. R., & Skinner, C. H. (2000). Randomized interdependent group contingencies: Group reinforcement with a twist. *Psychology in the Schools, 37*, 523-533.

Kratochwill, T. R., & Stoiber, K. C. (2002). Evidence-based interventions in school psychology: Conceptual foundations of the *Procedural and Coding Manual of Division 16 and the Society for the Study of School Psychology Task Force. School Psychology Quarterly, 17*, 341-389.

Lew, M., Mesch, D., Johnson, D. W., & Johnson, R. (1986). Positive interdependence, academic and collaborative-skills group contingencies and isolated students. *American Educational Research Journal, 23*, 341-347.

Litow, L., & Pumroy, D. K. (1975). A brief review of classroom group-oriented contingencies. *Journal of Applied Behavior Analysis, 8*, 341-347.

Myerson, J., & Hale, S. (1984). Practical implications of the matching law. *Journal of Applied Behavior Analysis, 17*, 367-380.

Page, D. P., & Edwards, R. P. (1978). Behavior change strategies for reducing disruptive classroom behavior. *Psychology in the Schools, 15*, 413-418.

Paine, S. C. (1983). *Structuring your classroom for academic success.* Champaign, IL: Research Press.

Popkin, J., & Skinner, C. H. (2003). Enhancing academic performance in a classroom serving students with serious emotional disturbance: Interdependent group contingencies with randomly selected components. *School Psychology Review, 32*, 282-295.

Rhymer, K. N., Skinner, C. H., Henington, C., D'Reaux, R. A., & Sims, S. (1998). Effects of explicit timing on mathematics problem completion rates in African-American third-grade elementary students. *Journal of Applied Behavior Analysis, 31*, 673-677.

Rhymer, K. N., Skinner, C. H., Jackson, S., McNeill, S., Smith, T., & Jackson, B. (2002).The 1-minute explicit timing intervention: The influence of mathematics problem difficulty. *Journal of Instructional Psychology, 29*, 305-312.

Romeo, F. F. (1998). The negative effects of using a group contingency system of classroom management. *Journal of Instructional Psychology, 25*, 130-133.

Skinner, C. H., Belfiore, P. J., Mace, H. W., Williams, S., & Johns, G. A. (1997). Altering response topography to increase response efficiency and learning rates. *School Psychology Quarterly, 12*, 54-64.

Skinner, C. H., Belfiore, P. B., & Watson, T. S. (1995/2002). Assessing the relative effects of interventions in students with mild disabilities: Assessing instructional time. *Journal of Psychoeducational Assessment, 20*, 345-356. (Reprinted from *Assessment in Rehabilitation and Exceptionality, 2*, 207-220, 1995).

Skinner, C. H., Cashwell, C. S., & Dunn, M. (1996). Independent and interdependent group contingencies: Smoothing the rough waters. *Special Services in the Schools, 12*, 61-78.

Skinner, C. H., Cashwell, T. H., & Skinner, A. L. (2000). Increasing tootling: The effects of a peer monitored interdependent group contingency on students' reports of peers' prosocial behaviors. *Psychology in the Schools, 37*, 97-110.

Skinner, C. H., Neddenriep, C. E., Robinson, S. L., Ervin, R., & Jones, K. (2002). Altering educational environments through positive peer reporting: Prevention and remediation of social problems associated with behavior disorders. *Psychology in the Schools, 39*, 191-202.

Skinner, C. H., Wallace, M. A., & Neddenriep, C. E. (2002). Academic remediation: Educational application of research on assignment preference and choice. *Child & Family Behavior Therapy, 24*, 51-65.

Slavin, R. E. (1987). Cooperative learning: Where behavioral and humanistic approaches to classroom management meet. *The Elementary School Journal, 88*, 29-37.

Stage, S. A., & Quiroz, D. R. (1997). A meta-analysis of interventions to decrease disruptive classroom behavior in public education settings. *School Psychology Review, 26*, 333-368.

Stoiber, K. C., & Kratochwill, T. R. (2000). Empirically supported interventions and school psychology: Rationale and methodological issues-Part I. *School Psychology Quarterly, 15*, 75-105.

Theodore, L. A., Bray, M. A., Kehle, T. J., & Jenson, W. R. (2001). Randomization of group contingencies and reinforcers to reduce classroom disruptive behavior. *Journal of School Psychology, 39*, 267-277.

Turco, T. L., & Elliott, S. N. (1990). Acceptability and effectiveness of group contingencies for improving spelling achievement. *Journal of School Psychology, 28*, 27-37.

Upson, L. M., & Skinner, C. H. (2002). A demonstration of class-wide data-based problem solving. *Inquiry: Critical Thinking Across the Disciplines, 21*(4), 41-49.

Van Houten, R., & Thompson, C. (1976). The effects of explicit timing on math performance. *Journal of Applied Behavior Analysis, 9*, 227-230.

Van Houten, R., Hill, S., & Parsons, M. (1975). An analysis of a performance feedback system: The effects of timing and feedback, public posting, and praise upon academic performance and peer interaction. *Journal of Applied Behavior Analysis, 12*, 581-591.

Using Interdependent Group Contingencies with Randomly Selected Criteria and Paired Reading to Enhance Class-Wide Reading Performance

Shannon R. Sharp
Christopher H. Skinner

University of Tennessee

SUMMARY. An intact second-grade class of 13 African-American students had completed few chapter-book reading assignments. A consultant worked with their teacher to develop an intervention that consisted of paired readings and two interdependent group contingencies. Following the implementation of the program, all students began reading chapter-books and the number of chapter-book quizzes passed increased from an average of less than 0.70 per week during baseline to 7.5 per week during the intervention phase. Discussion focuses on using interdependent group contingencies when targeting academic performance. *[Article copies available for a fee from The Haworth Document Delivery Service:*

Address correspondence to: Christopher H. Skinner, PhD, The University of Tennessee, College of EHHS, Claxton Complex A-518, Knoxville, TN 37996-3452 (E-mail: cskinne1@utk.edu).

[Haworth co-indexing entry note]: "Using Interdependent Group Contingencies with Randomly Selected Criteria and Paired Reading to Enhance Class-Wide Reading Performance." Sharp, Shannon R., and Christopher H. Skinner. Co-published simultaneously in *Journal of Applied School Psychology* (The Haworth Press, Inc.) Vol. 20, No. 2, 2004, pp. 29-45; and: *Single-Subject Designs for School Psychologists* (ed: Christopher H. Skinner) The Haworth Press, Inc., 2004, pp. 29-45. Single or multiple copies of this article are available for a fee from The Haworth Document Delivery Service [1-800-HAWORTH, 9:00 a.m. - 5:00 p.m. (EST). E-mail address: docdelivery@haworthpress.com].

http://www.haworthpress.com/web/JAPPS
Digital Object Identifier: 10.1300/J008v20n02_03

1-800-HAWORTH. E-mail address: <docdelivery@haworthpress.com>
Website: <http://www.HaworthPress.com> © 2004 by The Haworth Press, Inc.
All rights reserved.]

KEYWORDS. Reading comprehension, randomly selected criteria, interdependent group contingencies, pair readings, empirical case study

School psychologists have become involved in preventing and remedying academic skills deficits (Shapiro, 1996). Reading skill deficits are more common than any other academic skills deficits (Snow, Burns, & Griffin, 1998). Students who have difficulty reading are likely to experience learning problems across content areas (e.g., history, mathematics, literature) grade levels, and throughout their vocational careers (National Institute of Child Health and Human Development, 2000).

Educators and researchers have developed numerous interventions that have been shown to be effective for enhancing reading skills (Daly, Chafouleas, & Skinner, 2004; Hargis, 1999; National Institute of Child Health and Human Development, 2000). None of these interventions are likely to be effective unless students choose to participate or engage in reading behaviors associated with these interventions (Greenwood, Delquadri, & Hall, 1984; Skinner, 2002). Reinforcement programs have been shown to increase the probability of students choosing to read, the amount students read, reading fluency, and reading comprehension (Eckert, Ardoin, Daly, & Martens, 2002; Maheady, Sainato, & Maitland, 1983; Skinner, Skinner, & Armstrong, 2000; Trovato & Bucher, 1980).

Reinforcement typically involves establishing target behaviors, criteria, and consequences for meeting criteria. While reinforcement programs have been shown to be effective, educators may find it difficult to implement reinforcement programs for reading behaviors on a class-wide basis. One difficulty is associated with setting an academic performance criterion (Skinner, Williams, & Neddenriep, in press). In many educational settings, independent group-oriented contingencies are in place that target academic responding. The group-oriented characteristics of these contingencies include using the same target responses (e.g., read pages 12-17 and answer the questions on page 18), criteria (e.g., 70%-79% = C, 80-89% = B), and consequences (e.g., letter grades, if you make less than 70% must correct for homework) for each student. Each student's access to the consequence(s) is contingent upon his or her own performance and therefore *independent* of peers' behavior. Perhaps because students, parents, educators, and administrators consider them fair, independent group-oriented contingencies are often used for assigning grades and other consequences for academic behavior such as being required to enroll in extended school year programs or receiving an academic honor (Skinner, Skinner, & Sterling-Turner, 2002).

When using independent group-oriented contingencies it is difficult to set a common criterion across all students that will occasion each student's best performance (Litow & Pumroy, 1975). For example, skilled readers may require less time and effort to meet the criterion for earning reinforcement than less skilled readers (Skinner, Wallace, & Neddenriep, 2002; Stanovich, 1986). Basic and applied research on choice behavior suggests that both the additional effort and the thinner schedule of reinforcement (i.e., they meet the criterion less frequently and/or spend more time reading in order to meet the criterion), decreases the probability of less skilled readers choosing to engage in assigned reading behavior (Billington & Ditommaso, 2003; Billington, Skinner, Hutchins, & Malone, 2004; Neef, Mace, Shea, & Shade, 1992; Neef, Shade, & Miller, 1994). Thus, the students who most need to engage in assigned reading activities in order to remedy their skills deficits may be the least likely to choose to engage in these assignments (Skinner, 1998). Instead, less skilled readers may engage in other behaviors that require less effort and/or are associated with stronger reinforcement such as engaging in disruptive behaviors in order to obtain peer or teacher attention and engaging in passive off-task behaviors (flipping through pages, pretending to be reading silently) that allow them to escape and avoid reading.

Several solutions to this problem include altering contingencies for students with weaker reading skills by (a) lowering the performance criterion, (b) assigning easier work, and (c) providing stronger reinforcement for less skilled readers (Billington & Skinner, 2002; Cates, Skinner, Watkins, Rhymer, McNeill, & McCurdy, 2001; Cooke, Guzaukas, Pressley, & Kerr, 1993; Kern, Childs, Dunlap, Clarke, & Falk, 1994). Lowering the criterion and making assignments easier may be appropriate when students are misplaced in their curricula (Stanovich, 1986). However, in other instances, this merely amounts to lowering expectations and watering down the curricula, which may decrease learning rates (Roberts & Shapiro, 1996). Strengthening reinforcement (e.g., higher quality reinforcers, reinforce more often for less reading behavior) may cause these students to engage in assigned reading behaviors (Billington & Ditommaso, 2003). However, such procedures may cause social-behavioral problems and peers may complain that it is unfair that their classmates earn more or higher quality reinforcers for doing the same or less work (Axelrod, 1973; Turco & Elliott, 1990). Interdependent group contingencies may allow educators to address these problems associated with setting academic performance criteria across students with diverse levels of skill development (Skinner, Cashwell, & Dunn, 1996).

With interdependent group reinforcement all class members receive access to reinforcement contingent upon the group's behavior meeting a group-oriented criterion (e.g., class average). These contingencies are often included in cooperative learning programs that have been shown to enhance students' academic performance (Slavin, 1991). Interdependent group reinforcement programs may cause students to help one another succeed in order to increase the probability of all students earning reinforcement (Slavin, 1987). Because all-or-none of the students receive access to reinforcement, social-behavior problems such as reinforcer stealing and students labeling peers who do not receive access to reinforcement as dumb may be reduced (Cashwell, Skinner, Dunn, & Lewis, 1998). Students who rarely receive reinforcement for their individual behavior can share in the excitement of meeting a class goal (Skinner et al., 1996). Finally, educators may find such programs acceptable because they are effective (Stage & Quiroz, 1997) and resource efficient (Turco & Elliott, 1990).

As with other contingencies, it is difficult for educators to set an appropriate criterion. If the criterion is set too high, the group may not even attempt to earn the reinforcement. If the criterion is set too low, the students may merely do enough to earn access to reinforcement (Skinner et al., 2000). While baseline data can help teachers select a criterion, there is no way to ensure that a criterion based on baseline data is most appropriate (Popkin & Skinner, 2003). Randomly selecting group-oriented criteria may allow educators to avoid setting an inappropriate group criterion (Skinner et al., 1996). With this procedure, a criterion is not established prior to implementing the intervention. Instead, several criteria are developed and after student responding is completed a criterion is randomly selected. If the group meets or exceeds this criterion, they earn access to reinforcement.

While using randomly selected criteria has been recommended (Skinner et al., 1996), only three studies have employed such procedures when using group contingencies. In two of these studies researchers adapted the good behavior game and showed how randomly selecting criteria and/or target behaviors could be used to decrease inappropriate behaviors (Kelshaw-Levering, Sterling-Turner, Henry, & Skinner, 2000; Theodore, Bray, Kehle, & Jenson, 2001). In a third study, Popkin and Skinner (2003) showed how randomly selecting academic performance criteria and target behaviors could be used to enhance class-wide spelling, mathematics, and English performance.

Paired reading procedures also can encourage reading. Traditionally, the paired reading technique has consisted of a highly structured form of tutoring provided by a non-professional where specific guidelines regarding the level and nature of assistance provided by the tutor are followed (e.g., Greenwood, Delquadri, & Carta, 1997; Topping, 1988; Topping & Lindsay, 1992). Research on paired reading tutoring programs has shown gains in reading comprehension, reading fluency, and attitudes toward reading for peer tutees as well as peer tutors (Cupolillo, Silva, Socorro & Topping, 1997; Greenwood, Delquadri, & Hall, 1989; Topping, 1987).

The current study describes the development and evaluation of a class-wide intervention program consisting of less structured paired readings with two interdependent group contingencies designed to enhance reading performance in a second-grade classroom. The paired readings procedures technique used in the current study was relatively unstructured. This procedure was used to allow peers to encourage each other to read and help one another understand the material. One interdependent group contingency included a fixed criterion that required each student to pass at least one chapter book quiz. The other group contingency was implemented more frequently and the group-oriented criteria were randomly selected.

METHODS

Participants

Participants in this study were 14 African-American students (five girls and nine boys) from a second-grade classroom in an elementary school in the South Eastern U.S. Students were between 7 and 9 years old. The school's curriculum facilitator referred this class to a consultant because of concerns over the students' lack of interest in reading chapter-books. The consultant was a graduate student in her final year of coursework in a behavioral School Psychology Ph.D. program. The teacher was a 26-year-old female in her third year of teaching.

Setting

Procedures were run in the students' second grade classroom. During lessons, the students were seated at individual desks and the layout of the students' desks changed regularly throughout the year. During sustained silent reading time, approximately .5 hours per day, the children were allowed to find a quiet space on the floor to sit and read chapter-books from the Accelerated Reader (Renaissance Learning, 2002) program. If the students began talking to one another, they were instructed to move to a space that was more secluded.

Materials

The school used the Accelerated Reader (AR) program (Renaissance Learning, 2002). This program was developed to encourage students to read books, while giving teachers the ability to track the reading progress of individual students as well as the class as a whole. The student first selects from over 50,000 published books. Quizzes, which assess the student's level of reading comprehension through multiple-choice questions, have been developed for these books. When a student has completed a book, he or she takes the quiz for that book using computer software developed for this program. The computer then calculates the student's score based on the number of questions answered correctly, and awards points based on the difficulty of the text.

For the purposes of this study, the points were not used. Instead the number of quizzes passed (60% accuracy) served as the primary dependent variable. The computer program provides a table that can be individualized for each student, listing each book for which the student took a quiz, the date the quiz was taken, the number of questions answered correctly, and the number of points awarded.

Design, Baseline Phase, and Dependent Variable

An empirical case study consisting of an A-phase and a B-phase was used to evaluate the effects of the intervention. During baseline, typical classroom procedures were followed. Students received formal reading instruction from the teacher. Also they were encouraged to read AR books, especially chapter-books, independently and take comprehension quizzes on those books. Quizzes were taken on the computer and students had only one opportunity to take each quiz. Students chose books to check out from the library during their weekly library period.

Students were encouraged to choose a book from their current reading level. The library contained over 100 books for each child's reading level. When they completed a book, they were allowed to return it to the library and choose another. Approximately 30 minutes was allotted daily for this reading. Additionally, if during a school day a student finished their independent seatwork assignments early, he or she was encouraged to read their book until the rest of the class completed their work.

Baseline data were obtained using the computer record that indicated chapter-book quizzes passed by each student and the date that they passed those quizzes. The computer tracked each student performance on chapter-book quizzes. A score of 60% correct or higher was considered a passing score. The consultant graphed the number of AR chapter-book quizzes passed each week for three weeks prior to intervention implementation. These data served as baseline.

Intervention Training

On Monday morning after the last baseline school day, the consultant and teacher described the intervention to the students. Students were told that they would initially be paired with a peer and each pair would need to select one chapter-book from the library during their Library period. With one exception, the teacher paired students based on their reading levels such that both students in a pair were reading at approximately the same level. The exception was made for a student with very poor reading skills. That student, an 8-year-old female, was paired with a student who was both her friend and a higher-level reader so that the peer could provide assistance (e.g., correcting misread words, reading aloud accurately and discussing the content to aid in understanding) to this student. The students were encouraged to choose a book at their reading level (the library contained over 100 books for each reading level) and also to choose a book where the library had two copies of the book available. Students were allowed to share one copy if only one was available.

The students were then told that during sustained silent reading time (approximately .5 hours per day) they would be required to find a quiet place on the floor to read their chapter-book with their partner. The students were instructed to take turns reading with their partner, alternating each page, and to help each other read difficult words. After a pair finished reading a chapter-book, each student would take the AR quiz on that book. If both students passed the quiz, the pair would be given the option to either continue reading as a pair or continue reading independently.

Next the teacher described the two interdependent group contingencies. The first contingency had a fixed criterion and the second had a cumulative criterion that was randomly selected. The two contingency programs ran concurrently.

Fixed Criteria. Students were told that if each student passed at least one AR quiz within 6 weeks that the teacher would provide an ice cream party for the entire class. However, if even one student did not reach this goal, no students would receive ice cream.

Randomly Select Criteria. Next, the teacher described the second interdependent group contingency program that included randomly selecting group-oriented criteria or goals. Students were told that each Friday, the teacher would draw a slip of paper out of a bag. There were 13 slips of paper with numbers ranging from one to thirteen. Students were shown the bag and the slips of paper. If, during that week, the class had passed chapter-book quizzes totaling the number drawn or passed more quizzes than the number drawn, the whole class would receive an extra .5 hour of outside free time that Friday afternoon, but that they would get no extra free time if the class passed fewer quizzes than the number drawn.

Intervention Implementation

The intervention began immediately after the contingencies were explained to the students on Monday. While the students read in pairs, the teacher monitored the class to make sure that the students were alternating who was reading. If the students were found talking to other pairs, they were asked to move to a more secluded area. After a pair completed a book, each student independently completed the AR comprehension quiz. After a passing score (i.e., 60% or higher) was obtained by both students in the pair, the two students could choose to continue reading as a pair or to read independently.

The randomized interdependent group contingency occurred each Friday during the intervention phase. Using the computer software, the teacher obtained the number of AR chapter-book quizzes passed by each student in the class on that particular week. A random number was then drawn out of a paper bag (ranging from 1 to 13) and if at least that number of quizzes had been passed that week, the entire class was given an extra half hour of free time. To increase enthusiasm for the program by ensuring the students earned the reinforcement the first week, the teacher surreptitiously altered the slips of paper in the criterion bag so that all 13 slips contained the number 6; the number of chapter-book quizzes the students actually passed. Due to school closings and teacher absence, resulting in no reading time for several days, "week 4" of the intervention included 5 school days across 2 consecutive weeks.

On Monday of the third week, and each week thereafter, the teacher reminded students (in private) if they still had not yet passed a chapter-book quiz. At the end of the 6 weeks, data provided by the AR computer program indicated that the class goal was attained. As a result, on the last day of the intervention, the entire class participated in an ice cream party.

Treatment Integrity

The consultant observed the teacher implement the agreed-upon intervention plan at least two times per week. Additionally, the consultee was instructed to contact the consultant via e-mail if any problems arose. Neither the consultant's observations nor teacher reports indicated any problems with program implementation.

RESULTS

Figure 1 displays the number of chapter-book quizzes passed by the class each week during baseline and intervention phases. During baseline, the mean number of chapter-book quizzes passed each week was .67. During the intervention phase the mean number of chapter-book quizzes passed increased to 7.5 per week. Effect size was calculated by dividing the difference between the intervention and baseline means by the standard deviation during baseline (Busk & Serlin, 1992). Results show a large effect size of 12.37. Figure 1 shows an immediate and sustained increase (from one to six per week) in the class's rate of passing chapter-book quizzes after the intervention was implemented. During the final three weeks of the intervention phase, the class's number of chapter-book quizzes passed increased to an average of over 9 per week.

Table 1 displays each student's performance during baseline and intervention phases. During baseline only two chapter-book quizzes were passed, both by the same student (Student 9). The number of chapter-book quizzes passed by each student during the intervention phase was highly variable (range from one to seven), with over half of the

FIGURE 1. Number of AR Chapter-Book Quizzes Passed by the Class Each Week

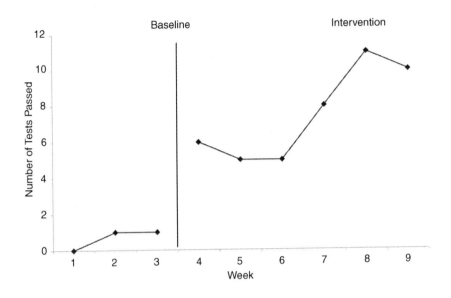

class (i.e., seven students) passing five or more quizzes, while four students (Student 2, 4, 8, and 12) only passed one quiz. Table 1 shows that the class met the fixed criterion contingency, as each student passed at least one quiz within 6 weeks.

DISCUSSION

The purpose of the current study was to evaluate the effects of a class-wide intervention on students' chapter-book reading performance. The computer generated data showed a large increase in chapter-book quizzes passed immediately after the intervention was implemented and an increasing trend as the intervention continued. These results suggest that the intervention was effective in increasing class-wide reading performance. However, before any strong conclusions can be drawn, future researchers should address several limitations associated with this study.

There are serious threats to internal validity associated with the current study that prevent one from drawing cause and effect conclusions.

TABLE 1. Number of AR Chapter-Book Quizzes Passed for Each Student During Baseline and Intervention Phases.

Student	Baseline	Intervention
1	0	6
2	0	1
3	0	5
4	0	1
5	0	5
6	0	7
7	0	3
8	0	1
9	2	5
10	0	5
11	0	2
12	0	1
13	0	3
Total	2	45

Although the current study includes a baseline phase, an intervention phase, empirical data, and statistical support (i.e., large effect size), the A-B design used to evaluate the intervention does not control for threats to internal validity. Therefore, as with other unscientific research methods (e.g., action research, qualitative research), the current study does not allow one to conclude that the intervention caused the change in class-wide reading performance.

Even if threats to internal validity had been controlled, because the intervention employed multiple components, it would not be possible to conclude which components caused the change. The enhanced reading performance could have been caused by (a) the paired readings procedure, (b) the fixed criterion group contingencies, (c) the randomly selected criteria contingencies, and/or (d) some interaction among these components. Future researchers should employ experimental designs (e.g., withdrawal design) to establish a cause and effect relationship between the intervention and the change in reading performance and component analysis procedures to identify which intervention component(s) caused the changes in reading performance.

The current study targeted one second-grade classroom containing 13 African-American students. Future researchers should assess the external validity of this intervention by replicating procedures across students, classes, target behaviors, ethnic groups, etc. In the current study, the class included only 13 students. Because interdependent group contingencies might not be as effective with larger groups (Hayes, 1976), future researchers investigating the external and educational or social validity of this intervention should consider running experimental studies in classrooms containing varying numbers of students.

In the current study, educators combined interventions in an attempt to reduce negative side effects associated with independent group contingencies. During baseline, the teacher was encouraging students to complete chapter-book quizzes and each student was receiving academic credit (e.g., their grade was enhanced) when they passed chapter-book quizzes. Baseline data showed that this was only mildly effective with one student. The teacher and consultant wanted to strengthen reinforcement for chapter-book reading, but were concerned about setting a criterion that would be too easy for some and too difficult for others. Employing randomly selected criteria addressed this concern. The teacher also was concerned that students who rarely met goals and received rewards for academic behaviors had given up. Using interdependent group contingencies addressed this concern because *all students* would receive access to reinforcers when the class met criteria. The teacher rigged the first week criterion selection so that the class would meet their goal. While Skinner et al. (1996) recommend doing this, they also caution educators not to rig the selection of criteria to ensure that students fail their goal.

Two other components of the intervention were added to ensure that each student felt as if he or she had made a contribution to the class's accomplishments. The intervention began with all students engaged in paired reading as opposed to isolated silent reading. This procedure increased the probability that students (a) with weaker reading skills, (b) who need higher rates of social interaction, and/or (c) who had difficulty with sustaining their reading would be more likely to experience success with their initial reading attempts. The fixed criterion was included to encourage pairs to work together to help one another pass at least one quiz. Results suggest that these procedures were effective because each student passed at least one chapter-book quiz, therefore helping the group earn the ice cream party. After each pair had passed their first chapter-book quiz, over half of the class (four pairs), including the pair with the strong and weak reader, continued reading together. This suggests that some students found chapter-book reading more acceptable when they engaged in paired reading.

When the consultant visited the room approximately 4 weeks after the consultation ended, she found that the teacher was continuing to run the randomized group contingency. Additionally, as per the consultant's recommendation, she had periodically altered the criteria pool by eliminating lower numbers (e.g., 1-5 quizzes passed per week) and adding higher numbers (14-18 quizzes passed per week). These data suggested that the teacher found this intervention acceptable. Furthermore, the students appeared to enjoy the program. During the intervention they often discussed the program and reported to peers, the teacher, and the consultant the number of chapter-book quizzes they had recently completed.

While the results of the current study are generally supportive, the fact that four students only passed one chapter-book quiz suggests that this intervention was not very effective with each student. The students' teacher indicated that these were four of her weaker readers. Perhaps the intervention was not strong enough to influence poor readers to choose to read. Alternatively, these students may not have had the prerequisite reading skills to pass the comprehension quizzes. Regardless, future research is needed to identify variables (e.g., students' current level or reading skill development) which allow educators to determine instances when this or similar interventions are most likely to be effective.

CONCLUSION

Educators and researchers have been working to identify specific interventions that have been shown to be effective for enhancing academic skill development (Kratochwill & Stoiber, 2000; National Institute of Child Health and Human Development, 2000). Once identified, these interventions can then be implemented by educators to prevent and remedy learning and behavior problems. Educators in the current study did not employ an empirically validated intervention program. Instead, the teacher and consultant applied previous theory and research to develop their own intervention to address the teacher's context specific needs and concerns. Thus, the current study serves as an example of how educators can be more than consumers of empirically validated interventions; they also can contribute to the prevention and remediation process by developing and evaluating their own interventions designed to address their own idiosyncratic concerns.

Although we have developed number curricula, strategies, and procedures designed to prevent and remedy reading skills deficits (Daly et al.,

2004), none are likely to be successful unless the students choose to read. Research on choice behavior suggests that students with reading skill deficits are less likely to choose to read than students with stronger reading skills (Billington et al., 2004; Skinner, 1998). The current study suggests that the practitioner-developed intervention that included paired reading and two types of interdependent group contingencies increased the probability of students choosing to read. Clearly, future scientific research is needed to empirically validate the effects of the current interventions and determine if this procedure can be used to enhance students' reading skills.

REFERENCES

Axelrod, S. (1973). Comparison of individual and group contingencies in two special classes. *Behavior Therapy, 4,* 83-90.

Billington, E. J., & Ditommaso, N. M. (2003). Demonstrations and applications of matching theory in education. *Journal of Behavioral Education, 12,* 91-104.

Billington, E. J., & Skinner, C. H. (2002). Getting students to choose to do more work: Evidence of the effectiveness of the interspersal procedure. *Journal of Behavioral Education, 11,* 105-116.

Billington, E. J., Skinner, C. H., Hutchins, H., & Malone, J. C. (2004). Varying problem effort and choice: Using the interspersal technique to influence choice towards more effortful assignments. *Journal of Behavioral Education, 13,* 193-207.

Busk, P.L., & Serlin, R.C. (1992). Meta-analysis for single-case research. In T. R. Kratochwill & J. R. Levin (Eds.), *Single case research design and analysis: Applications in psychology and education* (pp. 187-212). Hillsdale, NJ: Earlbaum.

Cashwell, C. S., Skinner, C. H., Dunn, M., & Lewis, J. (1998). Group reward programs: A humanistic approach. *Humanistic Education and Development, 37,* 47-53.

Cates, G. L., Skinner, C. H., Watkins, C. E., Rhymer, K. N., McNeill, B. S., & McCurdy, M. (2001). Effects of interspersing additional brief math problems on student performance and perception of math assignments: Getting students to prefer to do more work. *Journal of Behavioral Education, 9,* 177-193.

Cooke, N. L., Guzaukas, R., Pressley, J. S., & Kerr, K. (1993). Effects of using a ratio of new items to review items during drill and practice: Three experiments. *Education and Treatment of Children, 16,* 213-234.

Cupolillo, M., Silva, R., Socorro, S., & Topping, K. (1997). Paired reading and Brazilian first-year school failures. *Educational Psychology in Practice, 13,* 96-100.

Daly, E. J., Chafouleas, S., & Skinner, C. H. (2004). *Interventions for Reading Problems: Designing and Evaluating Effective Strategies.* Guilford Publications. Practical Intervention in the Schools.

Eckert, T. L., Ardoin, S. P., Daly, E. J., & Martens, B. K. (2002). Improving oral reading fluency: A brief experimental analysis of combining an antecedent intervention with consequences. *Journal of Applied Behavior Analysis, 35,* 271-281.

Greenwood, C. R., Delquadri, J., & Carta, J. J. (1997). *Together we can! Classwide peer tutoring to improve basic academic skills.* Longmont, CO: Sopris West.

Greenwood, C. R., Delquadri, J., & Hall, R. V. (1989). Longitudinal effects of classwide peer tutoring. *Journal of Educational Psychology, 81,* 371-383.

Greenwood, C. R., Delquadri, J., & Hall, R. V. (1984). Opportunity to respond and student academic performance. In W. L. Heward, T. E. Heron, J. Trap-Porter, & D. S. Hill (Eds.), *Focus on behavior analysis in education* (pp. 58-88). Columbus, OH: Charles Merrill.

Hargis, C. H. (1999). *Teaching and testing in reading: A practical guide for teachers and parents.* Springfield, IL: Charles C. Thomas.

Hayes, L. A. (1976). The use of group contingencies for behavior control: A review. *Psychological Bulletin, 83,* 628-648.

Kelshaw-Levering, K., Sterling-Turner, H. E., Henry, J. R., & Skinner, C. H. (2000). Randomized interdependent group contingencies: Group reinforcement with a twist. *Journal of School Psychology, 37,* 523-534.

Kern, L., Childs, K. E., Dunlap, G., Clarke, S., & Falk, G. D. (1994). Using assessment-based curricular intervention to improve the classroom behavior of a student with emotional and behavioral challenges. *Journal of Applied Behavior Analysis, 27,* 7-19.

Kratochwill, T. R., & Stoiber, K. C. (2000). Uncovering critical research agendas for school psychology: Conceptual dimensions and future directions. *School Psychology Review, 29,* 591-603.

Litow, L., & Pumroy, D. K. (1975). A brief review of classroom group-oriented contingencies. *Journal of Applied Behavior Analysis, 8,* 341-347.

Maheady, L., Sainato, D. M., & Maitland, G. (1983). Motivated assessment: The effects of extrinsic rewards on the individually-administered reading test performance of low, average, and high IQ students. *Education and Treatment of Children, 6,* 37-46.

National Institute of Child Health and Human Development (2000). *Report of the National Reading Panel. Teaching children to read: An evidenced-based assessment of the scientific research literature on reading and its implications for reading instruction* (NIH Publication No. 00-4769). Washington, DC: U.S. Government Printing Office.

Neef, N. A., Mace, F. C., Shea, M. C., & Shade, D. (1992). Effects of reinforcer rate and reinforcer quality on time allocation: Extension of matching theory to educational settings. *Journal of Applied Behavior Analysis, 25,* 691-699.

Neef, N. A., Shade, D., & Miller, M. S. (1994). Assessing the influential dimensions of reinforcers on choice in students with serious emotional disturbance. *Journal of Applied Behavior Analysis, 27,* 575-583.

Popkin, J., & Skinner, C. H. (2003). Enhancing academic performance in a classroom serving students with serious emotional disturbance: Interdependent group contingencies with randomly selected components. *School Psychology Review, 32,* 282-295.

Renaissance Learning. (2002). *Accelerated reader: Learning information system for reading and literacy systems.* Wisconsin Rapids, WI: Author.

Roberts, M. L., & Shapiro, E. S. (1996). Effects of instructional ratios on students reading performance in a regular education program. *Journal of School Psychology, 34,* 73-91.

Shapiro, E. S. (1996). *Academic skills problems: Direct assessment and intervention (2nd ed.).* New York: Guilford Press.

Skinner, C. H. (1998). Preventing academic skills deficits. In T. S. Watson & F. Gresham (Eds.). *Handbook of child behavior therapy: Ecological considerations in assessment, treatment, and evaluation* (pp. 61-83). New York: Plenum.

Skinner, C. H. (2002). An empirical analysis of interspersal research: Evidence, implications and applications of the discrete task completion hypothesis. *Journal of School Psychology, 40,* 347-368.

Skinner, C. H., Cashwell, C. S., & Dunn, M. (1996). Independent and interdependent group contingencies: Smoothing the rough waters. *Special Services in the Schools, 12,* 61-78.

Skinner, C. H., Skinner, A. L., & Armstrong, K. (2000). Shaping leisure reading persistence in a client with chronic schizophrenia. *Psychiatric Rehabilitation Journal, 24,* 52-57.

Skinner, C. H., Skinner, A. L., & Sterling-Turner, H. E. (2002). Best practices in contingency management: Application of individual and group contingencies in educational settings. In A. Thomas & J. Grimes (Eds.), *Best Practices in School Psychology* (4th ed., pp. 817-830). Washington, DC: The National Association of School Psychologists.

Skinner, C. H., Wallace, M. A., & Neddenriep, C. E. (2002). Academic remediation: Educational application of research on assignment preference and choice. *Child & Family Behavior Therapy, 24,* 51-65.

Skinner, C. H., Williams, R. L., & Neddenriep, C. E. (in press). Using Interdependent Group-Oriented Reinforcement to Enhance Academic Performance in General Education Classrooms. *School Psychology Review.*

Slavin, R. E. (1987). Cooperative learning: Where behavioral and humanistic approaches to classroom management meet. *The Elementary School Journal, 88,* 29-37.

Slavin, R. E. (1991). Cooperative learning and group contingencies. *Journal of Behavioral Education, 1,* 105-116.

Snow, C. E., Burns, S. M., & Griffin, P. (1998). *Preventing reading difficulties in young children.* Washington, DC: National Academy Press.

Stage, S. A., & Quiroz, D. R. (1997). A meta-analysis of interventions to decrease disruptive classroom behavior in public education settings. *School Psychology Review, 26,* 333-368.

Stanovich, K. E. (1986). Matthew effects in reading: Some consequences of individual differences in the acquisition of literacy. *Reading Research Quarterly, 21,* 360-406.

Theodore, L. A., Bray, M. A., Kehle, T. J., & Jenson, W. R. (2001). Randomization of group contingencies and reinforcers to reduce classroom disruptive behavior. *Journal of School Psychology, 39,* 267-277.

Topping, K.J. (1987). Peer tutored paired reading: Outcome data from ten projects. *Educational Psychology, 7,* 133-145.

Topping, K.J. (1988). Peer tutoring of reading using paired reading. *Educational and Child Psychology, 5,* 24-28.

Topping, K. J., & Lindsay, G. A. (1992). The structure and development of the paired reading technique. *Journal of Research in Reading, 15,* 120-136.

Trovato, J., & Bucher, B. (1980). Peer tutoring with or without home-based reinforcement for reading remediation. *Journal of Applied Behavior Analysis, 13,* 129-141.

Turco, T. L., & Elliott, S. N. (1990). Acceptability and effectiveness of group contingencies for improving spelling achievement. *Journal of School Psychology, 28,* 27-37.

A Self-Modeling Intervention
for High School Students
with Public Speaking Anxiety

Kristine A. Rickards-Schlichting
Thomas J. Kehle
Melissa A. Bray

University of Connecticut

SUMMARY. The study investigated the effectiveness of self-modeling as an intervention for public speaking anxiety. The participants were six high school students with elevated levels of self-reported public speaking anxiety. Students presented public speeches to randomly selected peer audiences. Direct observations measured the behavioral manifestations of public speaking anxiety. In the intervention phase, students viewed self-modeling videotapes that were edited to remove speech dysfluencies and behavioral symptoms of speech anxiety. The self-modeling tapes depicted only adaptive, exemplary behavior with an edited-in audience feature making it appear that the students were producing a fluent speech to an audience of their peers. All of the participants evidenced substantial decreases in behavioral symptoms of speech anxiety and these changes were

---

Address correspondence to: Thomas J. Kehle, Department of Educational Psychology, University of Connecticut, Storrs, CT 06269-2064 (E-mail: Thomas.Kehle@uconn.edu).

[Haworth co-indexing entry note]: "A Self-Modeling Intervention for High School Students with Public Speaking Anxiety." Rickards-Schlichting, Kristine A., Thomas J. Kehle, and Melissa A. Bray. Co-published simultaneously in *Journal of Applied School Psychology* (The Haworth Press, Inc.) Vol. 20, No. 2, 2004, pp. 47-60; and: *Single-Subject Designs for School Psychologists* (ed: Christopher H. Skinner) The Haworth Press, Inc., 2004, pp. 47-60. Single or multiple copies of this article are available for a fee from The Haworth Document Delivery Service [1-800-HAWORTH, 9:00 a.m. - 5:00 p.m. (EST). E-mail address: docdelivery @haworthpress.com].

47

maintained throughout follow-up. The range of the participants' effect sizes was 2.7 to 4.9. Self-report measures of state anxiety and confidence as a speaker were used to assess additional effects of treatment. For all participants, there were also substantial decreases in self-reported public speaking anxiety and state anxiety from baseline to follow-up. A post-treatment interview revealed high social validity and self-reported generalization of treatment. *[Article copies available for a fee from The Haworth Document Delivery Service: 1-800-HAWORTH. E-mail address: <docdelivery@haworthpress.com> Website: <http://www.HaworthPress.com>* © 2004 by The Haworth Press, Inc. All rights reserved.]*

KEYWORDS. Self-modeling, anxiety, public speaking, adolescents, communication

Fears about speaking in public are not uncommon. A recent survey found that 30% of the respondents experienced excessive anxiety when they spoke to a large audience (Stein, Walker, & Forde, 1996). Additionally, 10% of the respondents reported that the excessive anxiety had produced extreme interference in different contexts such as work, social life, and educational pursuits. It was also found that public speaking anxiety (PSA) peaked between the ages of 13 and 17 or the high school years (Stein et al., 1996). How individuals communicate with each other defines how we perceive ourselves, how others perceive us, and how accessible we are to learning in the classroom (Hurt & Preiss, 1978; McCroskey, Daly, Richmond, & Falcione, 1977). The purpose of this study was to determine the effectiveness of a self-modeling intervention on high school students' PSA, as measured with behavioral indices and self-reports of anxiety, using an ABA design.

Self-modeling is defined as "an intervention procedure using the observation of images of oneself engaged in the adaptive behavior" (Dowrick, 1999, p. 23). Specifically, videotapes are edited to depict exemplary-only behavior. The participants, as part of a training or therapy program, view their respective videotapes over several occasions. The self-observation of these tapes has been shown to promote desired therapeutic effects (Dowrick, 1999; Kahn, Kehle, Jenson, & Clark, 1990).

Self-modeling treatments have been applied with positive results to a myriad of behaviors including stuttering (Bray & Kehle, 1996; Bray & Kehle, 1998), anxiety and depression (Dowrick & Jesdale, 1990; Kahn et al., 1990), and selective mutism (Kehle, Owen, & Cressy, 1990;

Kehle, Madaus, Barratta, & Bray, 1998). However, apparently only one study exists that employed self-modeling in a school setting to attenuate public speaking anxiety (Germaine, 1983). In this study, the students were videotaped on their first day of speech class and then the tapes were edited to exclude speech dysfluencies. The participants viewed their edited videotapes over four sessions and observers evaluated the speeches pre- and post-treatment for dysfluencies. It was found that the treatment was effective for participants with measured low self-esteem, but treatment was not beneficial for participants with measured high self-esteem. In fact, participants with high self-esteem evidenced a decrease in their self-esteem scores after viewing the videotapes. Germaine (1983) specified that this study "indicated support for raised self-efficacy as the component of self-modeling responsible for behavioral change" (p. 1) and further suggested that superior quality self-modeling videos may be needed to create significant changes for individuals with PSA.

Viewing the edited, self-modeling tapes may serve to increase the individual's belief in their ability to speak fluently and confidently in public, and this increase in self-efficacy could lead to significant behavior change as well as other cognitive changes, such as a reduction of anxiety. Self-modeling treatments may also promote the generalization and maintenance of the behavior over time (Kehle, Clark, Jenson, & Wampold, 1986).

In summary, the purpose of the present study was to investigate the effects of a self-modeling intervention for adolescents with the intent of reducing the behavioral manifestations and anxiety associated with public speaking. In contrast to Germaine's (1983) study, the current study included self-modeling videotapes that depicted an edited-in audience feature, and the use of a state anxiety measure.

METHODS

Participants and Setting

Six general education high school students (male = 5, female = 1) were selected to participate in the study. The students were recruited from four elective classes at a suburban New England high school. Five of the students were Caucasian and one student was of Indian/ Asian ethnic descent. The selected participants met the following criteria: (1) parental consent; (2) high PSA as measured by the Personal Report of Public Speaking Anxiety (84th percentile or 1 standard deviation above the mean); (3) no previous instruction in public speaking;

(4) no involvement in special education; (5) not currently taking any psychiatric medication; and (6) not receiving treatment from a psychologist/therapist, psychiatrist, or speech pathologist.

The peer audience consisted of 30 high school students who had parental consent and were recruited from three elective classes. Participants and audience members were instructed that their participation made them eligible for two pizza parties at the end of the study. The peer audience was randomly selected for each speech in order to control for familiarization effects. An audience of 5 to 25 peers attended all the baseline and follow-up phases.

Experimental Design

An ABA design replicated across six students was employed due to constraints of scheduling within the school day and Board of Education policies. Although AB designs are arguably the most common treatment designs employed by practicing school psychologists, they are often mistakenly assumed to preclude valid inferences regarding causality. However, Kazdin (1982) and Kratochwill (1992) have convincingly argued for the validity of AB designs when they meet specific conditions. Kazdin stated that AB designs could provide valid conclusions inferred from the data if the following conditions are met: (1) data are objective; (2) there are multiple assessment occasions; (3) the problem is stable; (4) there is an immediate and pronounced intervention effect, and (5) the participants are heterogeneous. Similarly, Kratochwill also noted valid inferences can be deduced from AB designs if the study was planned (vs. *expost facto*), the treatment was standardized and possessed integrity, and large effect sizes were realized.

The present study met all of the above conditions and therefore threats to internal validity were substantially negated. The ABA design employed in this study included observation only at the baseline and follow-up phases. The intervention phase consisted of the participants viewing their respective edited intervention tapes; further, in concert with the Germaine (1983) study, no public speaking with corresponding measurement of PSA was conducted. However, the primary reason for this was simply the real time constraints of the students' educational programs. If data were collected during the intervention phase, it would have entailed the additional replacement of scheduled curriculum with public speaking presentations for both the participants and peer audience. The measure of PSA during follow-up allowed sufficient inference, in accordance with Kazdin (1982), to insure that the cause of change was due to treatment.

Dependent Variables/Instrumentation

Direct Observation. Collection of direct observational data across baseline and follow-up was conducted via videotaped recordings of the student's speeches. All the speeches were rated using the Behavioral Assessment of Speech Anxiety (BASA) measure with repeated 1-minute sweeps for each observation session (Mulac & Sherman, 1974). The BASA measure is comprised of 18 scales for the purpose of measuring the behavioral manifestations of speech anxiety that may be observed during a speaking performance. The major variables of measured behavior include tone of voice, verbal fluency, stress of mouth and throat, facial expression, arm and hand movement, overall bodily movement, and an overall anxiety estimate. Trained observers used the measure and rated all the items in 1-minute sweeps. Each scale is quantified for the level of anxiety observed on a Likert scale with the range of "no anxiety at all" recorded as a 0 to "strong anxiety" recorded as a 9. Each of the 18 scales has assigned variable weights and the weighted scores of the specified variables can be combined to create four independent dimensions of speech anxiety. The factors are "Rigidity," "Disfluency," "Inhibition," and "Agitation." Mulac and Sherman reported .95 reliability ratings for the instrument's total weighted scores. On each of the 18 variables, separate reliability estimates ranged from .70 to .96. The median reliability estimate for the instrument was .84. Validity of the instrument was determined by correlating the mean of "overall speech anxiety" scores with the total BASA scores. The Pearson-product moment correlation for the two measurements was .88. A coefficient of determination of .77 reflected that the two measures share over three quarters of common variance.

Self-Reported Public Speaking Anxiety. Self-reported public speaking anxiety was used to measure the participants' levels of PSA at baseline and follow-up. The Personal Report of Public Speaking Anxiety (PRPSA) is a 34-item Likert-type scale that yields scores with a possible range of 34 to 170 (McCroskey, 1970). The hypothetical neutral position for the PRPSA is 102. This instrument was designed to measure public speaking anxiety conceptualized as generalized context communication apprehension. The PRPSA measures anxiety levels pertaining to public speaking and does not measure any other types of communication-based anxieties. McCroskey (1984) administered the Personal Report of Public Speaking Anxiety to 25,000 college students nationwide and it was reported that 5% had very low anxiety, 5% had moderately low anxiety, 20% had moderate anxiety, 30% had moderately high anxiety, and 40% had very high anxiety. It was found that the "normal" range for public speaking anxiety was in the moderately high to high ends, and that most people experience fear and stress when the situation calls for speaking in public.

The PRPSA was administered to 945 college undergraduates and internal reliability estimates for the measure were .94. A test-retest reliability estimate (N = 769) was .84 over a 10-day period. Additionally, an item analysis and factor analysis demonstrated that all the items loaded on a single factor and were discriminating. Richmond and McCroskey (1985) specified scores on the PRPSA to discriminate low (34-84), moderately low (85-92), moderate (93-110), moderate high (111-119), and very high (120-170) levels of public speaking anxiety. People with very high levels of public speaking anxiety were described as very likely to avoid public speaking situations due to the significant anxiety experienced. The PRPSA was recorded before the onset of the baseline phase and at post-treatment. The data were compared via visual inspection to observe if there was a relationship between treatment and the participant's level of self-reported public speaking anxiety.

Self-Reported State Anxiety. State anxiety was used to assess the level of anxiety experienced by the participants before and after treatment. The STAI-S (Form Y-1) is a 20-item instrument that measures how participants feel "right now, at this moment" (Spielberger, 1983). The scale measures anxiety-related feelings such as apprehension, tension, and worry. Changes in transitory anxiety due to treatments such as counseling, behavior modification, and psychotherapy have been successfully assessed with the STAI-S. Normative data on the STAI-S were available for high school students. Test-retest reliabilities for the STAI-S ranged from .34 to .62 and were expected to be low due to the transitory nature of the test. However, evidence of the internal consistency of the STAI-S was provided with the mean alpha reliability coefficient of .92. Overall, it was found that the reliability of the STAI-S increased when it was given after a stressful situation (Spielberger, 1983). Consequently, the STAI-S was administered after the first baseline speech and after the last follow-up speech for each participant. The data were compared via visual inspection to observe if there was a relationship between the treatment and the participant's level of self-reported state anxiety.

Data Collection

Baseline data, using the BASA, were collected on 5 occasions over a period of 3 weeks where it was required that each student present speeches to a peer audience. The students randomly chose speech topics from a "fishbowl" of topics, such as "please describe your favorite movie," "please talk about people that you admire," "what you would do if you were president," and "what do you think the differences are between boys and girls?" Subsequently, the students were given 2 minutes to compile their 3-minute speeches. Notes or any other prompters were not allowed. The students were randomly selected for the order in which they presented their speeches. Also, a randomly selected peer audience of approximately 5 to 20 volunteers attended all the baseline sessions. The PRPSA and STAI-S were administered immediately at the start of the baseline speech and at follow-up.

Self-Modeling Intervention Videotape Construction

The intervention tapes were created during baseline by videotaping the students presenting speeches on randomly selected topics on current events with only the examiner and the student in the room. Subsequently, an audience of the students' peers was edited in, making it appear that the student was speaking in front of an audience. The intervention tapes were also edited to exemplify behavior that was free from speech dysfluencies and other behavioral manifestations of speech anxiety as revealed by the BASA instrument.

During the intervention phase, the student and examiner privately met 5 times over a period of 3 weeks to view their respective self-modeling videotapes. The intervention meeting times were distributed with at least 1 day of no viewing between the intervention sessions in order to maximize the potential power of the spacing effect. Research on the spacing effect indicates that learning is maximized when presentations of material are interspersed, rather than massed together (Dempster, 1988).

The succession of steps for creating the self-modeling videotape was as follows:

1. The student was given the speech topic and allowed time for preparation.
2. The tape was edited to remove any behaviors representative of speech anxiety as recognized by the BASA instrument. The edited videotapes were 3-4 minutes in length.

3. Two 3-second segments of the student's peer audience were edited into the tape in order to give the appearance of the student presenting a public speech. One 3-second segment was placed approximately mid-way in the tape and showed the audience paying attention. The second 3-second audience clip was placed at the end of the tape and exhibited the peer audience clapping.

The follow-up phase of the study ensued approximately 1 month after the intervention phase had been completed. The follow-up phase closely followed the design of the baseline phase. Each participant was observed presenting a 3-minute speech on a randomly selected topic on 4 separate, spaced occasions, in front of a randomly selected peer audience. Again, the students were randomly selected as to which order they presented their speeches. Notes and prompters were not allowed and all the sessions were assessed with the BASA instrument. Immediately following the last follow-up speech, the STAI-S was administered. Lastly, the participants were assessed with the PRPSA.

Treatment Integrity

A treatment protocol was established in order to ensure treatment integrity. The treatment protocol was as follows: (1) Each 3-4 minute tape was viewed in its entirety; (2) The student watched their own videotapes; (3) No exchange of conversation between the experimenter and the participant took place when the tape was being viewed; and, (4) The days of viewing the intervention tape were spaced at least one day apart.

Inter-Observer Agreement

Two observers rated at least 25% of the videotaped direct observations across the two phases using the BASA measurement. The observers were trained how to use the BASA measure and inter-observer agreement was assessed by percent agreement. Each of the two observers viewed 7 sessions of the participants' public speaking exercises and completed the BASA measure for each session. The BASA score of the experimenter was compared with the observer's BASA score for the same participant from the same session. Inter-observer agreement was derived by the division of the BASA score of the experimenter over the BASA score of the observer, then determining the percentage of that number. The range for the inter-observer agreement was 73% to 99%. The mean inter-observer agreement across the two phases was 81%.

Social Validity

Social validity was assessed by a follow-up student interview. Students met with the examiner a few weeks after the study had been completed. All students were asked the same questions and inquiries that included, "what was the most liked/least liked part of the program?" "do you think this experience will help you in the future? how?" and "what changes would you have made to the program?"

RESULTS

Direct Observation

As depicted in Figure 1, all 6 students evidenced a substantial decrease in the behavioral manifestations of public speaking anxiety from baseline to follow-up. During the baseline phase, the students' scores on the BASA were relatively stable. Effect sizes were calculated for each student using a method proposed by Busk and Serlin (1992). Specifically, their *Approach One: No Assumptions* method was used wherein the effect size for each student was derived by calculating the difference in the means of the baseline and follow-up phases, divided by the standard deviation of the student's baseline phase. Each data point depicted in Figure 1 represented the total summed score of the BASA measure for each 3-minute speech. The effect sizes are exhibited in Table 1 and range from 2.7 to 4.9. A "small effect" was considered .20, a "medium effect" was .50, and a "large effect" was .80. Therefore, the effect sizes for all six students were in the large effect category. "The larger the effect size, the more consistent is the effect of the independent variable" (Heiman, 1996, p. 370).

Self-Reported Public Speaking Anxiety

Table 1 also depicts the participants' scores on the PRPSA at baseline and follow up. A decrease on this instrument indicates improvement in the individual's level of confidence regarding public speaking and, as depicted, all six students exhibited substantial improvement. Percent reduction was calculated for each student and the range for percent reduction was from 13% to 41% indicating that the participants felt more comfortable and skilled in public speaking forums at the post-treatment phase.

Self-Reported State Anxiety

Also depicted in Table 1 are the baseline and follow-up scores on the STAI- S across the participants. A decrease in scores on the STAI-S refers to a reduction in state anxiety. The percentage reduction in STAI-S ranged from 21 to 55.

FIGURE 1

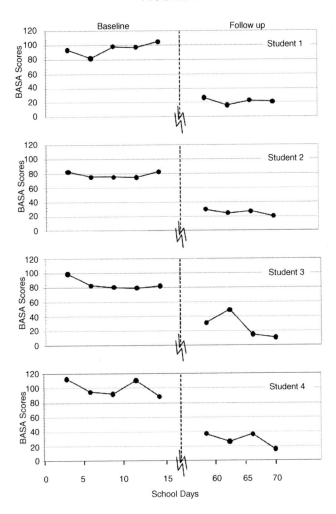

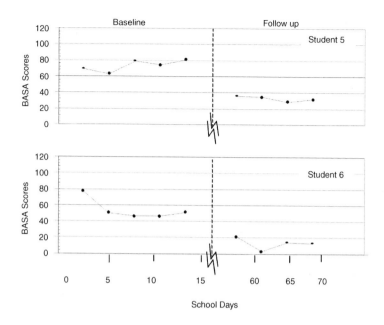

TABLE 1. Effect Sizes on the BASA, and Percent Reduction of Participants' Scores on the PRPSA, and STAI-S from Baseline to Follow-Up.

	Student					
	1	2	3	4	5	6
Effect size on the BASA	4.9	3.6	3.9	4.7	2.7	2.7
Percent reduction on the PRPSA	23	21	13	34	13	41
Percent reduction on the STAI-S	48	37	43	40	21	55

Social Validity

All students were interviewed at follow up about the intervention. The students were all asked the same set of questions and met individually with the examiner. In summary, all of the students expressed very positive support for the intervention across the questions asked. In addition, the teacher noted that the students exhibited dramatic positive changes in their public speaking ability.

DISCUSSION

The use of self-modeling as a treatment was dramatically successful in reducing the behavioral manifestations of public speaking anxiety for all six students. As noted in Figure 1, the effect of the intervention was pronounced and immediate. After the first follow-up speech, all the students' scores on the BASA dropped substantially and the positive trend continued throughout the follow-up phase.

All six students experienced decreases in self-reported state anxiety, as measured by the STAI-S, and increases in self-reported confidence as a speaker, as measured by the PRPSA. Although state anxiety and public speaking confidence were not directly targeted in the self-modeling intervention, by the nature of editing out speech anxious behaviors, the tapes depicted the students as being less anxious and more confident.

Finally, although AB designs are not typically considered experimental designs, "under some circumstances, uncontrolled case studies may be able to provide information that closely approaches that which can be obtained from experimentation" (Kazdin, 1982, p. 88). The study was designed to include the conditions outlined by Kazdin (1982) and Kratochwill (1992) that allowed for valid inferences to be drawn from the self-modeling intervention. These conditions involved implementing a standardized treatment with fidelity that permitted observation and collection of objective and stable data over multiple assessment occasions. Further, the results were immediate and pronounced, and evident across diverse participants. These conditions essentially eliminated threats to the internal validity of the study such as, practice effects, instrumentation, and statistical regression. Public speaking anxiety has a very stable course over time and has shown to be resistant to treatment (McCroskey, 1977; McCroskey, Anderson, Richmond, & Wheeless, 1981), thereby strengthening the claim that the self-modeling intervention was the causal agent and the results were not due to history, maturation, or repeated testing (Kazdin, 1982; Kratochwill, 1992).

In conclusion, self-modeling is an effective intervention for a myriad of persistent problematic behaviors that have been historically resistant to change. Although the implementation of a self-modeling intervention is time-consuming for the interventionist, it requires little of the participant's time. The only equipment needed is a video camera and editing equipment. The first step in conducting a self-modeling intervention is to obtain a videotape of reliable baseline behavior. This baseline tape is then edited using either analog or digital equipment that is commonly available in the schools. The participant views the edited intervention videotape depicting exemplary behavior, such as fluent public speaking, on five or six spaced occasions over a period of several weeks. As is most common in school-based interventions, an AB research design would be employed. The degree of improvement relative to the baseline can be determined graphically or by calculating effect sizes.

Limitations

The results in this study cannot be generalized to a population of individuals with public speaking anxiety and the conclusions about the effectiveness of this treatment are confined to the treatment sample. However, single subject designs can explore many research questions with individuals or groups (Kazdin, 1982) and are practical measures for use in school systems and clinical settings. In addition, external validity in single subject design can be substantiated through replication.

REFERENCES

Bray, M. A. & Kehle, T. J. (1996). Self-modeling as an intervention for stuttering. *School Psychology Review*, *25*, 358-369.

Bray, M. A. & Kehle, T. J. (1998). Self-modeling as an intervention for stuttering. *School Psychology Review*, *27*, 585-596.

Busk, P. L. & Serlin, R. C. (1992). Meta-analysis for single-case research. In T. R. Kratochwill & J. R. Levin (Eds.), *Single-case research design and analysis: Applications in psychology and education* (pp. 187-212). Hillsdale, NJ: Lawrence Erlbaum Associates.

Dempster, F. N. (1988). The spacing effect: A case study in the failure to apply the results of psychological research. *American Psychologist*, *43*, 627-634.

Dowrick, P. W. (1999) A review of self-modeling and related interventions. *Applied and Preventative Psychology*, *8*, 23-39.

Dowrick, P. W. & Jesdale, D. C. (1990). Effects sur l' emotion de la retransmission video structuree: Implication therapeutiques [Effects on emotion of structured video replay: Implications for therapy]. *Bulletin de Psychologie*, *43*, 512-517.

Germaine, K. A. (1983). *Self-esteem as a variable in the efficacy of self-modeling*. Unpublished master's thesis, University of Alaska-Anchorage.

Heiman, G. W. (1996). *Basic statistics for the behavioral sciences* (2nd edition). Boston: Houghton Mifflin Company

Hurt, H. T. & Preiss, R. (1978). Silence isn't necessarily golden: Communication apprehension, desired social choice, and academic success among middle school students. *Human Communication Research*, *4*, 315-328.

Kahn, J. S., Kehle, T. J., Jenson, W. R., & Clark, E. (1990). Comparison of cognitive-behavioral, relaxation, and self-modeling interventions for depression among middle school students. *School Psychology Review*, *19*, 196-211.

Kazdin, A. (1982). *Single-case research designs*. New York: Oxford University Press.

Kehle, T. J., Clark, E., Jenson, W. R., & Wampold, B. E. (1986). Effectiveness of self-observation with behavior disordered elementary school children. *School Psychology Review*, *15*, 289-295.

Kehle, T. J., Madaus, M. R., Baratta, V. S., & Bray, M. A. (1998). Augmented self-modeling as a treatment for children with selective mutism. *Journal of School Psychology, 36,* 247-260.

Kehle, T. J., Owen, S. V., & Cressy, E. T. (1990). The use of self-modeling as an intervention in school psychology: A case study of an elective mute. *School Psychology Review, 19,* 115-121.

Kratochwill, T. R. (1992). Single-case research design and analysis: An overview. In T. R. Kratochwill & J. R. Levin (Eds.), *Single-case research design and analysis* (pp. 1-14). Hillsdale, NJ: Lawrence Erlbaum Associates.

McCroskey, J. C. (1970). Measures of communication bound anxiety. *Speech Monographs, 37,* 269-277.

McCroskey, J. C. (1984). The communication apprehension perspective. In J. A. Daly & J. C. McCroskey (Eds.), *Avoiding communication: Shyness, reticence, and communication apprehension* (1st edition). Beverly Hills, CA: Sage.

McCroskey, J. C., Andersen, J. F., Richmond, V. P., & Wheeless, L. R. (1981). Communication apprehension of elementary and secondary students and teachers. *Communication Education, 30,* 122-132.

McCroskey, J. C., Daly, J. A., Richmond, V. P., & Falcione, R. L. (1977). Studies of the relationship between communication, apprehension, and self-esteem. *Human Communication Research, 3,* 267-277.

Mulac, A. & Sherman, A. R. (1974). Behavioral assessment of speech anxiety. *Quarterly Journal of Speech, 60,* 134-143.

Richmond, V. P. & McCroskey, J. C. (1985). *Communication apprehension, avoidance, and effectiveness* (1st edition). Scottsdale, AZ: Gorsuch Scarisbrick.

Spielberger, C. D. (1983). *The State-Trait Anxiety Inventory-Form Y.* Redwood City, CA: Mindgarden.

Stein, M. B., Walker, J. R., & Forde, D. R. (1996) Public-speaking fears in a community sample. *Archives of General Psychiatry, 53,* 169-174.

Use of Delayed Praise as a Directive and Its Effectiveness on On-Task Behavior

Dorothy M. Trolinder

Hee-sook Choi

Theron B. Proctor

University of South Dakota

SUMMARY. This study investigated the effectiveness of delayed, directive praise on the on-task behavior of children identified as having a low level of attention. Utilizing an A-B-A-B single subject design, each child received delayed praise, employed as a directive for future behavior, from his or her classroom teacher during the treatment phases. The on-task behavior of each participant rose substantially between the initial baseline and treatment conditions and remained elevated throughout the study. Similarities between student performances suggest that students with low on-task behavior respond positively to delayed, directive praise and that the positive effects of such praise generalize over time. *[Article copies available for a fee from The Haworth Document Delivery Service: 1-800-HAWORTH. E-mail address: <docdelivery@haworthpress.com> Website: <http://www.HaworthPress.com> © 2004 by The Haworth Press, Inc. All rights reserved.]*

Address correspondence to: Hee-sook Choi, PhD, Associate Professor, Program Coordinator of School Psychology, Division of Counseling & Psychology in Education, School of Education, University of South Dakota, 414 East Clark Street, Vermillion, SD 57069 (E-mail: hchoi@usd.edu).

[Haworth co-indexing entry note]: "Use of Delayed Praise as a Directive and Its Effectiveness on On-Task Behavior." Trolinder, Dorothy M., Hee-sook Choi, and Theron B. Proctor. Co-published simultaneously in *Journal of Applied School Psychology* (The Haworth Press, Inc.) Vol. 20, No. 2, 2004, pp. 61-83; and: *Single-Subject Designs for School Psychologists* (ed: Christopher H. Skinner) The Haworth Press, Inc., 2004, pp. 61-83. Single or multiple copies of this article are available for a fee from The Haworth Document Delivery Service [1-800-HAWORTH, 9:00 a.m. - 5:00 p.m. (EST). E-mail address: docdelivery@haworthpress.com].

KEYWORDS. Delayed praise, effectiveness, on-task behavior, withdrawal design

Classroom interventions to improve attention to curricular tasks have historically included cognitive-behavioral techniques, designed to teach problem-solving strategies; medications, designed to increase attention and decrease excess activity; and behavioral management techniques, designed to reinforce task-focused behavior while decreasing inappropriate behaviors (Kronenberger & Meyer, 2001). While cognitive-behavioral interventions have demonstrated some effectiveness with executive functions such as problem-solving strategies, the extensive teacher time required to train students to use the strategies paired with low generalization across settings limits its application. Thus, cognitive-behavioral techniques have not received widespread support as classroom-based interventions for specific cognitive skills such as attention (DuPaul & Stoner, 1994; Frazier & Merrell, 1997).

Perhaps the most effective single treatment, psychostimulant medications often improve attention and reduce impulsivity, overactivity, restlessness, and aggressiveness (Kronenberger & Meyer, 2001; Rosenberg, Hoittum, & Gershon, 1994; Wiener, Jaffe, Goldstein, & Justice, 1996). However, about 25% of children diagnosed with ADHD fail to respond to psychostimulants (Barkley, 1998). Moreover, some children develop undesirable side effects such as nausea, decreased appetite, weight loss, headaches, crying, increased heart rate, retarded growth rate, or addiction (Kronenberger & Meyer, 2001; Rosenberg, Hoittum, & Gershon, 1994; Wiener, Jaffe, Goldstein, & Justice, 1996).

Frequently used in general and special education classrooms, behavior modification programs incorporate a variety of reinforcement and punishment responses as a means of eliciting desired behaviors from children. Positive reinforcement, a widely used class of responses to student behavior (Frazier & Merrell, 1997), often incorporates techniques such as token economies, contingency contracting, and shaping. Though the efficacy of these techniques is well documented for increasing attention, behavioral interventions can be lengthy and intensive and require considerable teacher attention and consistency for implementation and monitoring (Frazier & Merrell, 1997; Kronenberger & Meyer, 2001; Pfiffner & Barkley, 1998). Behavioral interventions such as token-based economies in the classroom are also frequently criticized by educators because using tangible reinforcers tend to increase student reliance on external sources of reinforcement (Deci, 1975; Deci & Ryan, 1980, 1985).

Historically, praise has been an effective form of positive reinforcement for students. Unlike tokens, praise does not involve a tangible reinforcer, costs the teacher little time, and may be used at anytime. Verbal-direct praise, defined as a direct statement to the student that he or she is engaging in inappropriate behavior (Kronenberger & Meyer, 2001), has been linked to increased motivation to perform an activity (Butler, 1987; Deci, 1972; Cameron & Pierce, 1994; Deci, 1971; Koestner, Zuckerman, & Koestner, 1987), eliciting more frequent student response (Khan, 1998), and increased on-task behavior (Houghton, Wheldall, Jukes, & Sharpe, 1990). Because praise provides information to the student about his or her performance in regards to a standard, it allows the recipient to alter his or her performance to more closely approximate the teacher's expectations (Delin & Baumeister, 1994; Carton, 1996).

Considerable research has documented the effects of praise as a reinforcer with normal students. However, students with attentional deficits often require more structure and additional cues to perform at their optimal level. Barkley (1997, 1998) suggests children with attentional difficulties demonstrate difficulty maintaining task persistence and task vigilance. These children tend to perform better in environments that provide external sources of behavioral motivation, including external prompts, cues, reminders, or physical props. Moreover, their performance increases when provided with immediate, brief, consistent, salient, and more frequent rewards. All of which suggests that, despite its merits, the use of praise alone in the classroom for students with attention problems might not be effective in increasing their on-task behavior.

Given that most education services for children with attentional difficulties occur in the regular classroom, including those diagnosed with Attention Deficit Hyperactivity Disorder (ADHD), regular education teachers can benefit from effective and easy-to-implement interventions for children with attention problems. Considering the relentless demand placed upon the regular education teacher's time and attention, it is no surprise that teachers tend to use praise that is infrequent, noncontingent, and global (Brophy, 1981). Within this context, the current study evaluates a cost- and time-efficient way for classroom teachers to use praise to encourage on-task behavior for students with attention problems who might otherwise miss out on significant classroom instruction.

Using praise as a directive that is delivered later at a specific point in time may be an effective intervention technique particularly for children with attentional difficulties. Delaying praise provides the teacher an opportunity to use the positive effects of praise in a more organized and structured fashion and, therefore, provides a directive for future student behavior. It incorporates the benefits of praise by providing encouragement, building both global and academic self-esteem, and contributes to a close teacher-student relationship (Brophy, 1981). The use of delayed praise as a directive further provides an external source of behavior motivation, structure, and consistency much needed for children with attentional difficulties, thus reducing the likelihood of noncontingent and global use of praise. It is simple to administer, time and cost efficient, and provides behavioral reinforcement. Since on-task behavior frequently replaces disruptive classroom behavior (Andrews & Kozma, 1990), delayed praise can provide a less distracting learning environment for all students. Therefore, the purpose of this study was to investigate the effectiveness of delayed praise, used as a directive, on the classroom attention of elementary school students, identified by their teacher as having a low level of attention.

METHOD OF INVESTIGATION

Participants

Unlike younger children, adolescents are more likely to perceive praise as manipulative or embarrassing (Meyer, Bachmann, Biermann, Hempelmann, Ploger, & Spiller, 1979; Houghton, Wheldall, Jukes, & Sharpe, 1990). Thus, for this study elementary age students were chosen to decrease the likelihood of these confounding factors. Two second grade students and their teachers from an elementary school in a rural mid-west community were selected. The student participants were chosen by their teachers based on the teachers' perception that he or she demonstrated lower attention-to-task during academic activities than his or her classmates. In addition, a minimum T-score of 60 was set on the ADHD Index and the DSM-IV Total scales of the *Conner's Teacher Rating Scale-Revised: Long Version (CTRS-R:L)* to be eligible for the study. Both students met this criterion.

Teacher 1 had 20 years of teaching experience in the selected school district and had taught second grade for 16 years. Teacher 2 had seven years of teaching experience and was teaching second grade for the first time. Both teachers were female. An arbitrary decision was made to identify one teacher and student as Teacher 1 and Student 1, and the other pair as Teacher 2 and Student 2. Teacher 1 submitted the names of two students who fit the initial participant identification requirements. Teacher 2 proposed one student's name. Two students ultimately returned parental consent to school. Child 1 was an eight-year-old male student of Teacher 1. Child 2 was an eight-year-old female student in Teacher 2's class.

Instrumentation

In addition to the subjective referral, the teachers completed a *Connors' Teacher Rating Scale-Revised: Long Version (CTRS-R:L)* for the participating children. Conner (1997) suggests that T-scores above 60 on the CTRS-R:L indicate possible significant problems related to attention and/or hyperactivity. A T-score of 60 on both the ADHD Index and DSM-IV Total scales of the CTRS-R:L was, therefore, selected as a cut-off point. The ADHD Index score is the best indicator of whether a child is likely to have an attention problem (Conner, 1997). Elevated T-scores on the DSM-IV Symptoms subscale indicate the likelihood that an individual's attention or hyperactivity rises to a clinically significant level (Conner, 1997). Principally used as a tool in the assessment of ADHD, CTRS-R:L is also used as a screening measure, treatment-monitoring device, and as a research instrument (Barkley, 1998; Conners, 1997). It is intended to be completed by the classroom teacher who is familiar with the student's classroom behavior. As this research was performed well into the second semester of the school year, each teacher was believed to be familiar with her students.

The ADHD index of the CTRS-R:L contains 12 items that identify children at risk for ADHD diagnosis. The 18-item DSM-IV symptoms subscale links classroom behaviors to the American Psychiatric Association's Diagnostic and Statistical Manual of Mental Disorders (DSM-IV) (1994) diagnostic criteria. Teachers complete the 59-item survey by indicating the degree of difficulty the child has had in common problem areas over the past month. Responses are measured on a four-point Likert scale.

The overall internal reliability coefficients for the CTRS-R:L range from 0.773 to 0.958. For males between the ages of 6 and 11 the ADHD Index coefficients range from 0.942 to 0.943, and the coefficient of the DSM Total scale is 0.95. For similar age females, the ADHD Index coefficients range from 0.919 to 0.940, and the coefficient of the DSM Total scale ranges from 0.924 to 0.954. Test-retest reliability coefficients for the ADHD Index is 0.80 and for DSM-IV 0.63. The intercorrelation between the ADHD Index scale and DSM Total scale for males is 0.97 and 0.96 for females.

A behavior observation sheet for the purpose of recording the dependent variable, time on-task, was developed for this study (Appendix A). The rater used a point-time interval recording. Interval recording is a recording method whereby the presence or absence of a predefined target behavior is recorded over a specified amount of time. When using point-time interval sampling, the rater records the presence or absence of a specific behavior during a specified portion of the time interval (Sattler, 2002).

The rater for this study rated behaviors as on-task or off-task for the first 10 seconds of each half-minute. That is, for each minute the rater observed and recorded behavior for the first 10 seconds, and between 30 and 40 seconds. Rating behaviors twice per minute was done for two reasons. First, the children selected for the study were, by definition, students with poor academic attention. More frequent recordings were thought to provide a better estimation of the child's actual on-task time. Second, as it was not necessary to record the behavior of non-participating students, the rater had the time available to rate the participant more frequently. Each observation occurred over a 20-minute interval, resulting in 40-recorded observations for each observation period.

Research Design

A single-subject experiment utilizing an A-B-A-B design was carried out for each participant over 16 school days. This design was selected as it is especially useful for evaluating the effect of an investigation on an individual basis and has high internal validity. The length of the study was established for practical reasons. First, the proposed length allowed for four equal phases of four days, which met the minimum standard of three days per phase suggested by Barlow and Hersen (1984). Additionally, the length of the study was limited in an attempt to minimize potential intrusiveness in the classroom. The A-B-A-B design was chosen to provide a better opportunity to compare the results of interventions that were provided to different students by different teachers in different settings and at different times. Several strategies were implemented to reduce possible forms of error and bias that might result from the research design.

Operationalizing the dependent variable, on-task behavior, and training the observer according to these parameters served to reduce measurement error. On-task behavior was operationalized in the following manner: (a) the student is seated at his or her desk or appropriate work-place; (b) the student's hands are manipulating only items necessary for the activity; and (c) the student's head is oriented toward the direction dictated by the activity. The child must exhibit all three components of on-task behavior to be considered on-task. In addition, five strategies were introduced to reduce the amount of researcher bias. First, an independent observer was used to observe and record the participant's behaviors. Second, the same observer performed all observations for both participants. Third, the lengths of the baseline and treatment stages were pre-established at four days per phase. Fourth, the observer remained blind to the purpose of the study. Finally, the researchers remained uninformed as to trends in the data during their collection.

Research Procedure

At a regular weekly meeting of the four second grade teachers at the selected elementary school, one of the researchers briefly explained the nature of the research including teacher time commitment, identification of potential student participants, and the projected benefits of participation. In addition to a personal invitation to participate in the study, each teacher received a letter that included information regarding the study and an informed consent form for voluntary participation. Participating teachers were then asked to consider students who demonstrate low attention-to-task during academic activities. That is, in the teacher's opinion the student demonstrates lower-than-average attention to task on classroom academic activities when compared to his or her classmates. Teachers were asked to exclude any students with a history of special services or obvious history of behavioral difficulties. It is more likely that such students have received or would be receiving special interventions, which would confound the results of the experiment.

Three of the four second grade teachers indicated initial interest in the project. The fourth teacher reported that none of her students met the student qualification of low attention to task. Follow-up appointments were made with each of the three interested teachers. During the individual meetings the research protocol was explained in further detail. Each teacher signed two copies of the consent, returning one to the researchers and retaining the other for her records. Teachers were then asked to submit the names of students who demonstrate low attention-to-task during academic activities. Teacher 1 submitted the names of two students who fit the initial identification requirements. Teachers 2 and 3 each proposed one student's name.

Teachers were then given a packet containing two copies of the Parent Information and Consent Form and asked to send the packet home with each respective child the next day. A researcher then contacted each family by telephone to explain the project and to invite their child to participate. Two children, one from Teacher 1's and one from Teacher 2's class, ultimately returned parental consent. Once parental permission was obtained, the classroom teachers completed the CTRS-R:L.

Child 1's Index scores were as follows: ADHD Index, 64; Global Index: Restless-Impulsive 70; Global Index: Total, 70, DSM-IV: Inattentive 63; DSM-IV Hyperactive-Impulsive 64; and DSM-IV: Total 64. Child 2's Index scores were as follows: ADHD Index 82; Global Restless-Impulsive 89; Global Index: Total 85; DSM-IV-Inattentive 72; DSM-IV: Hyperactive-Impulsive 73; and DSM-IV: Total, 76. Based on the ADHD Index and DSM-IV Total scales of the CTRS-R:L, both students met the qualifications for participation.

The independent observer and teachers attended separate training sessions provided by one of the researchers. The study utilized one observer, a male who had completed the coursework in school psychology and had one year of professional practice as a school psychologist. His training included instruction in the use of the Behavior Observation Sheet (Appendix A) and the time sampling technique as well as clarification of the operational definition of on-task behavior. Following didactic instructions and discussion, the observer practiced the observation technique by rating the on-task and off-task behaviors of students videotaped during classroom activities similar to those expected under experimental conditions. The researcher selected two five-minute segments of the video for the training. During each training segment the observer observed and recorded the on-task and off-task behaviors of a specified child.

Inter-rater reliability was obtained by a point-by-point agreement ratio between the observer and a researcher. This method of reliability scoring allows comparison of the scorers' agreement and disagreement on a point-by-point basis (Kazdin, 1982). Thus, if both raters score the behavior as occurring or not occurring for the same interval, an agreement is scored. Disagreement occurs when one rater scores a behavior as on-task and the other rater scores the same behavior, during the same interval, as off-task. The ratio is found by dividing the total number of agreements between the observers by the total number of agreements plus the disagreements for the trial, then multiplying that product by 100 to obtain a percentage (A/A + D × 100, where A = agreements between the observers and D = disagreements between the observers)

(Kazdin, 1982). Inter-rater reliability was 100% agreement for both five-minute time samplings. To check for possible rater drift the observer was recalled after the first two weeks of the study and his accuracy crosschecked with a previously unviewed portion of the videotape. Using point-by-point agreement ratio comparing the scoring of a researcher to that of the rater, the inter-rater reliability remained at 100%.

Due to the scheduling requirements of the volunteer teachers, two separate, but similar teacher training sessions were conducted. The training session began by thanking the teacher for her willingness to participate in the study. The purpose of the study was then reiterated. On-task behavior, as defined by the researchers was discussed. To reduce the potential for incorrectly judging behaviors as on- or off-task, each teacher was asked if the definition of on-task behavior met her current classroom standards. For example, one criterion defined in the protocol is that the student is seated at his or her desk or appropriate work place. As not all teachers require that his or her students be seated during academic activities, clarification of the current classroom management techniques was needed. Both teachers indicated the current parameters were congruent with her management style. When asked, neither teacher added any criterion to the existing definition of on-task behavior.

During training, careful attention was given to ensure that the teachers understood and could successfully make praise statements according to the research standard. Teachers were asked to include four elements into their praise statements: use of the student's name, a statement of appreciation, a specific description of the behavior being praised, and consideration, or a cue, toward a future goal. Teachers were instructed to continue their normal classroom method of recognizing students for appropriate behavior.

However, during the treatment phases they were to approach the child before the day's lesson and to deliver the appropriate praise regarding the child's previous day's performance in a face-to-face dialogue. Following presentation of several sample scripts containing appropriate praise statements, each teacher completed practice sessions using taped vignettes similar to those described for the observer-training session. Appendix B contains the teacher training agenda, including the sample praise statements. After a two-minute portion of the video, the tape was stopped and the teacher was asked to write a praise statement relevant to the situation, using the four elements of praise. The researcher reviewed the completed statement with the teacher to insure all the elements were included. Suggestions to improve the praise statements were made as needed. Four additional two-minute practice sessions were conducted in a similar manner. The teacher retained her copy of the sample praise statements for reference throughout the study.

Each teacher was also given a Praise Record form (Appendix C) upon which she was asked to record the praise statement she would plan to give to the child during the actual treatment phase. For reference purposes, the recommended content of a praise statement was printed on this form. For her convenience, each teacher was provided with a Delayed Praise Daily Schedule (Appendix D), which prompted the teacher to observe, write, and deliver praise statements as required.

The study commenced with Child 1. Child 2 was added four days later, following the baseline period for Child 1. During each daily session the rater observed and recorded the target student's behavior as on-task or off-task. The rater also indicated on the behavior observation sheet if a one-on-one interaction between the teacher and student occurred before the instructional activity. As it was believed the observer would not always be in a close enough physical proximity to hear the private teacher-student exchange, and to reduce possible interference in the classroom, the observer was asked to note only if the interaction occurred. According to the rater's data sheets, a teacher-student exchange occurred on each of the scheduled intervention days and not on the scheduled baseline days.

Observation of each participant was scheduled during language arts instruction because both teachers indicated this activity provided the most stable observational opportunities. That is, language arts instruction was scheduled every school day at a uniform time. Both teachers indicated that they provided language arts instruction during the morning session, between 10:15 and 11:30.

Each of the two baseline and two treatment conditions were scheduled for 4 consecutive daily sessions of 20 minutes. Other than the presence of the observer in the classroom, the teacher was requested to make no changes in her normal classroom routine during the baseline conditions. Specifically, she was asked to conduct her daily instructional activities and teacher-to-student interactions as she would if the observer was not present.

Beginning on the last day of the baseline condition (day 4) each teacher was instructed to note an on-task behavior demonstrated by the participant child during the language arts session. At the earliest opportunity after the behavior occurred, such as during a planning period or recess, the teacher was asked to record the praise statement she intended to deliver to the student. Writing down the intended praise allowed the teacher the opportunity to construct the appropriate components of praise into the statement, and served to later remind her of the observed on-task behavior. The teacher was requested to deliver the praise statement regarding the previous day's on-task behavior to the student in a private one-to-one interaction before the beginning of the next day's language arts lesson. Thus, praise for the behavior noted on day 4 was delivered on day 5. Praise for the behavior noted on day 5 was delivered on day 6, and so on for the duration of the treatment phase. Following the first 4-day treatment interval the teacher was asked to discontinue praising the student in the prescribed manner for the duration of the second 4-day baseline condition. After the second baseline condition, the second treatment condition, identical to the first treatment condition, began. Treatment and observation of the participant concluded after this condition.

Unless specified otherwise, all observation periods were for a 20-minute duration. All data for the first baseline condition was gathered at a consistent time for Child 1, and there were no extraneous or unexpected circumstances. On day 7 (treatment 1, day 3), according to the rater, the child was engaged in a conflict with another student during recess, which occurred before the language arts instruction period. On day 8 (treatment 1, day 4) language arts instruction occurred in the afternoon due to a morning field trip. Data was collected at that time. All of the second baseline observations occurred at a consistent time in the morning. On day 9 (baseline 2, day 1) the lesson included an art project. On day 14 (treatment 2, day 2) the rater noted Child 1 had "a clearly unique day," in that the child, in a joking way, behaved just the opposite of what the teacher requested of him. There was no obvious reason for the oppositional behavior. The child was absent from school on the scheduled day 15, so the second treatment phase was extended by one day. Due to standardized testing, which occurred during the morning hours, language arts instruction occurred in the afternoon on days 15 and 16 (treatment 2, days 3 and 4).

Baseline 1 and Treatment 1 data (days 1 though 8) were gathered for Child 2 at a consistent time. Due to a field trip on day 10 (baseline 2, day 2), language arts instruction occurred an hour later than normal, and the observer was able to make only 10 observations before the children left for lunch. On day 12 (baseline 2, day 4), Child 2's activities included writing an e-mail on the classroom computer, and working on a painting. Both of these hands-on activities were unusual during the observation period. Language arts instruction occurred in the afternoon on days 12 through 16 (baseline 2, day 4 through treatment 2, day 4) due to standardized testing, which occurred during the morning hours. The observer noted that the behavior of the entire class was "very boisterous" on day 15 (treatment 2, day 3). On day 16 (treatment 2, day 4) he noted that Child 2 did not seem to understand the assigned task, which was a workbook assignment.

Data Analysis

After the data was collected, the proportion of on-task behavior for each observation period was calculated by dividing the number of intervals the child was on-task by the total number of possible observations. With the exception of day 10 for Child 2, the total possible observations were 40. The total possible observations for the exceptional day were 10. Data for each child were then plotted in a simple line graph across separate phases of the study. Observation days are represented on the abscissa axis of the simple line graph. The dependent variable, percentage of on-task behavior, is represented on the ordinate axis (see Figure 1 & Figure 2). Data analysis included computing the mean percentages and visual inspection of the performance graphs of each participant to determine changes in the mean level during and between each treatment phase.

RESULTS

Figure 1 provides a graphic representation of the data from Child 1 over the course of all baseline and treatment conditions. During baseline 1 (B1), Child 1's on-task behavior ranged from 32.5% to 65% (M = 49.4, SD = 14.5). His on-task behavior during treatment condition 1 (T1) ranged from 67.5% to 82.5% (M = 73.1, SD = 5.69). Child 1's percentage of on-task behavior increased by an average of 23.7% between B1 and T1. During baseline 2 (B2), Child 1's on-task behavior ranged from 57.5% to 80% (M = 69.4, SD = 8.73). On average, his percentage of on-task behavior decreased by 3.7% between T1 and B2. For treatment condition 2 (T2), Child 1's on-task behavior ranged from 62.5% to 77.5% (M = 71.9, SD = 5.69). His on-task behavior rose by an average of 2.5% between B2 and T2.

Figure 2 provides a graphic representation of the data from Child 2 over the course of all baseline and treatment conditions. During baseline 1 (B1), Child 2's on-task behavior ranged from 40% to 72.5% (M = 56.3, SD = 13.97). Her on-task behavior ranged from 70% to 95% (M =

FIGURE 1. Student 1 On-Task Behavior Over the Course of Baseline and Intervention Conditions

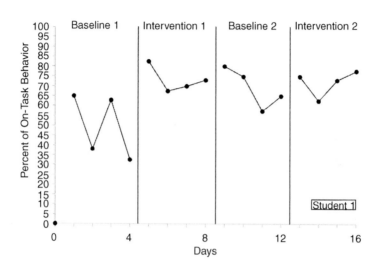

FIGURE 2. Student 2 On-Task Behavior Over the Course of Baseline and Intervention Conditions

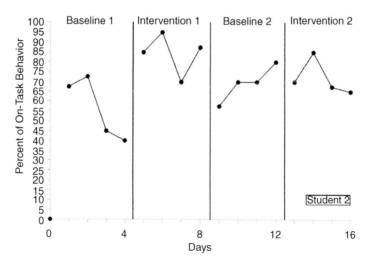

84.4, SD = 9.08) during treatment phase 1 (T1), resulting in an average increase of 28.1% from B1 to T1. Child 2's on-task behavior ranged from 57.5% to 80% (M = 69.4, SD = 7.98) during B2, resulting in an average decrease of 15% in on-task time between T1 and B2. During treatment condition 2, Child 2's on-task behavior ranged from 67.5% to 85% (M = 71.9, SD = 7.78). This reflects an average increase of 2.5% between B2 and T2.

Overall, following the onset of T1, Child 1 and Child 2's on-task behavior, on average, increased by about 24% and 28%, respectively. Child 1's on-task behavior fell about 4% and Child 2's about 15% between T1 and B2. Both of their on-task behaviors rose by an average of about 2.5% between B2 and T2. As expected, the on-task behavior of each student rose considerably during the first treatment condition. Child 1's on-task behavior then remained relatively high throughout the remainder of the study. Though Child 2's on-task behavior decreased somewhat from the first treatment phase to the second baseline phase, it failed to rise substantially during the last treatment phase. However, in comparison to the average rate of on-task behavior during B1 (M = 56.3), Child 2's on-task behavior rate during T2 (M = 71.9) was still fairly high.

DISCUSSION

On-task behavior for both participants rose significantly between the initial baseline and treatment conditions. Based on the level of behavior that was established by each student during the initial baseline phase, it can be said with some degree of confidence, that something about the delayed directive praise intervention resulted in behavioral change for each of the two participants. Even though the students were praised on different days, in separate environments, and by different teachers, not to mention their gender difference, the on-task behavior of each student rose upon implementation of the praise intervention. Obtaining similar responses across individuals, time, and settings suggests the effect of this type of praise might be generalizable. Practically speaking, this means that teachers can easily learn and implement a positive intervention that may produce swift behavioral responses for many students. This finding is especially important in the classroom setting, where the teacher's time is limited, and where the practical effects of increased attention can include increased learning and decreased disruptiveness.

As in all classrooms, many unexpected events occurred in each environment during the study. The observer stated that Child 1's fight at recess on day 7 seemed to distract the child during the observation period. The entire class of Child 2 was "very boisterous" on day 15, and Child 2 had difficulty understanding the workbook assignment on day 16. In addition, both classes went through the preparation and process of taking standardized tests. Each of these activities and events occurred during intervention phases of the study. Logically, these events might be expected to decrease on-task behavior. However, on average, the student's on-task behavior was higher during each of the intervention phases than during each child's initial baseline phase. On the other hand, the highest on-task behavior day for each child during a baseline condition occurred on days when favored activities like art and computer projects occurred. As expected, the student's on-task time was greater as they enjoyed favored activities.

There are several possible hypotheses as to why the behavior did not extinguish during the second baseline condition. First, the cognitive (Baumeister, Hutton, & Cairns, 1990; Cameron & Pierce, 1994; Carton, 1996; Delin & Baumeister, 1994), emotional (Brophy, 1981; Delin & Baumeister, 1994) motivational (Butler, 1987; Cameron & Pierce, 1994; Koestner, Zuckerman, & Koestner, 1987; Ryan, Mims, & Koestner, 1983), or interpersonal (Brophy, 1981) consequences of praise may have led to the generalization or transference of the behavior to non-treatment phases. In other words, the most obvious explanation for the sustained on-task behavior across the second baseline condition is that, at least in some children, the positive effects of praise may not be quickly extinguished. This may be because the students received information about the self and his or her performance (Carton, 1996), which increased attention to his or her performance (Baumeister, Hutton, & Cairns, 1990) or motivation to remain on-task (Butler, 1987).

Secondly the participants were recognized by their teachers as students with poor on-task behavior. Such students may be more accustomed to receiving redirection through reprimands than by positive cues. Therefore, praise may have acted as an encourager that prompted continued on-task behavior once the teacher discontinued the praise treatment. This is in line with the results of the study conducted by Houghton, Wheldall, Jukes, and Sharpe (1990) who found that improved on-task behavior was still evident two months after the praise intervention.

An alternative reason for the sustained on-task behavior is posed by Kazdin (1982), who suggested that a limitation of A-B-A-B designs is that the behavior change agent, in this case the teacher, may not revert to the baseline condition. It is possible that the study increased the teachers' consciousness of the students when they exhibited appropriate behavior. This awareness may have resulted in inadvertently praising behavior during non-observed or non-treatment conditions. Although the rater did not observe any inadvertent praise during his classroom observations, this could not be ascertained for non-observed instruction times. The possibility that it might have occurred is suggested by the following discourse. During training, both teachers indicated that including the four components of praise seemed unnatural, and that the practice sessions were helpful in that the practice forced them to become familiar with constructing appropriate praise statements. In follow-up interviews conducted after data collection was complete, each teacher reported that writing the daily praise statement on the Praise Record Form initially took more time as she learned to incorporate the four components. However, by the end of the study, constructing praise statements seemed natural. Each also reported that because of the study she now delivers student praise in a more personal and specific manner.

Research design related factors might also explain the results. The study was designed such that the length of each phase was predetermined. Experimental control within the study was not gained because the student's behavior did not return to the baseline level. It is possible that the phases were of too short a duration to allow the behavior to be extinguished during the return-to-baseline phase. This seems true especially for Child 1, whose on-task behavior for day 9 may have been related to a preferred activity, and whose on-task behavioral trend seems to be decreasing during the second baseline phase. The opposite may be true for Child 2 who displayed the highest on-task rate on day 12, the last day of second base line, due to a preferred activity, which might have interrupted the trend in decreased on-task behavior.

In short, the findings of the study indicated that delayed praise, used as a directive, initially increased the child's attention to task to a significant degree. Though reason for the sustained on-task behavior is unclear, in comparison to each child's initial baseline phase the child's on-task behavior was, on average, significantly higher during each of the intervention phases despite the unexpected events. More importantly, the initial increase in on-task behavior at a significant level across individuals, time, and settings suggests that the effect of delayed directive praise may be readily generalizable. Thus, the results clearly indicate that the use of delayed praise as a directive is an additional cost- and time-efficient way for classroom teachers to increase on-task behavior of children particularly with attentional difficulties. Moreover, this study demonstrates how teachers and school psychologists working together utilizing a single subject experimental design can evaluate the effectiveness of any planned interventions within the classroom setting.

Given the strong demand for accountability in the public schools for both teachers and school psychologists, this particular research design would seem invaluable for obtaining solid evidence to demonstrate that changes observed are a result of the intervention(s).

Finally, future research may consider using a multiple-baseline design across individuals. Though it is possible that the student's behavior failed to return to baseline level because the intervention resulted in long-term or permanent change, one way to assess an intervention while avoiding the reversibility requirement demanded by an A-B-A-B design would be employing a multiple-baseline design across individuals. In addition, this study considered the participant as being on task when he or she was at his or her appropriate work place, manipulating only appropriate materials, and looking toward the direction directed by the activity. Each teacher was asked to praise any appropriate behavior demonstrated by the student during the prescribed time. It was up to the teacher to determine which specific behavior she wanted to reinforce on any given day. Thus, there was no way to determine specifically if any one behavior was better or worse on any given day. Future studies might address a single and specific behavior such as being in one's seat or consider a multiple-baseline design across behaviors if each participant's on-task behavior is actually deemed multiple behaviors. Furthermore, it would be worthwhile to obtain some measure of academic performance to examine the relationship between increased on-task behavior and academic progress. A final suggestion for future study involves monitoring the classroom behavior of the teachers. In the current study two different teachers obtained similar results with two different students. It may be helpful to examine how or if the teachers' attitudes toward the students were altered as a result of participation in the study.

REFERENCES

American Psychiatric Association. (1994). *Diagnostic and statistical manual of mental disorders* (4th ed.). Washington, DC: Author.

Andrews, L., & Kozma, A. (1990). Increasing teacher praise and altering its distribution to children of differing on-task levels. *Canadian Journal of Behavioral Science*, 22(2), 110-120.

Barkley, R.A. (1997). Attention deficit-hyperactivity disorder. In E.J. Mash & R.A. Barkley (Eds.) *Treatment of childhood disorders* (pp. 38-72). New York: Guilford.

Barkley, R.A. (1998*). Attention-deficit hyperactivity disorder: A handbook for diagnosis and treatment.* Guilford Press, New York.

Barlow, D.H., & Hersen, M. (1984). *Single case experimental designs.* New York: Pergamon Press.

Baumeister, R. F., Hutton, D. G., & Cairns, K. J. (1990). Negative effects of praise on skilled performance. *Basic and Applied Social Psychology, 11,* 131-148.

Brophy, J. (1981). Teacher praise: A functional analysis. *Review of Educational Research, 51,* 5-32.

Butler, R. (1987). Task-involving and ego-involving properties of evaluation: Effects of different feedback conditions on motivational perceptions, interest, and performance. *Journal of Educational Psychology, 79,* 474-482.

Cameron, J., & Pierce, D. (1994). Reinforcement, reward, and intrinsic motivation: A meta-analysis. *Review of Educational Research, 64,* 363-423.

Carton, J. S. (1996). The differential effects of tangible rewards and praise on intrinsic motivation: A comparison of cognitive evaluation theory and operant theory. *The Behavior Analyst, 19,* 237-255.

Conners, C. K. (1997). Conners' rating scales-revised technical manual. *Multi-Health Systems:* New York.

Deci, E.L. (1971). Effects of externally mediated rewards on intrinsic motivation. *Journal of Personality and Social Psychology, 18,* 105-115.

Deci, E.L. (1972). Intrinsic motivation, extrinsic reinforcement, and inequity. *Journal of Personality and Social Psychology, 22,* 113-120.

Deci, E.L. (1975). *Intrinsic motivation.* New York: Plenum.

Deci, E. L., & Ryan, R. M. (1980). The empirical exploration of intrinsic motivational processes. In L. Berkowitz (Ed.), *Advances in experimental social psychology* (pp. 39-80). New York: Academic Press.

Deci, E.L., & Ryan, R.M. (1985). *Intrinsic motivation and self-determination in human behavior.* New York: Plenum.

Delin, C.R., & Baumeister, R.F. (1994). Praise: More than just social reinforcement. *Journal for the Theory of Social Behavior, 24,* 219-241.

DuPaul, G.J., & Stoner, G. (1994). *ADHD in the schools: Assessment and intervention strategies.* New York: Guilford.

Frazier, M.R., & Merrell, K.W. (1997). Issues in behavioral treatment of attention-deficit/hyperactivity disorder. *Education and Treatment of Children, 20,* 441-461.

Houghton, S., Wheldall, K., Jukes, R., & Sharpe, A. (1990). The effects of limited private praise on classroom behavior in four British secondary school classes. *British Journal of Educational Psychology, 60,* 255-265.

Kazdin, A.E. (1982). *Single-case research designs.* New York: Oxford Press.

Khan, Z. (1998). *The effect of classroom teacher praise on the frequency of discourse on an underachieving student.* Unpublished doctoral dissertation. University of South Dakota.

Koestner, R., Zuckerman, M., & Koestner, J. (1987). Praise, involvement and intrinsic motivation. *Journal of Personality and Social Psychology, 53,* 383-390.

Kronenberger, W. G., & Meyer, R. G. (2001). *The child clinician's handbook* (2nd ed.). Boston: Allyn and Bacon.

Meyer, W., Bachmann, M., Biermann, U., Hempelmann, M., Ploger, F., & Spiller, H. (1979). The informational value of evaluative behavior: Influences of praise and blame on perceptions of ability. *Journal of Educational Psychology, 71,* 259-268.

Pfiffner, L. J., & Barkley, R. A. (1998). Treatment of ADHD in school settings. In R. A. Barkley, *Attention-Deficit Hyperactivity Disorder* (pp. 458-490). New York: Guilford.

Rosenberg, D. R., Hoittum, J., & Gershon, S. (1994). *Textbook of pharmacology for children and adolescent psychiatric disorders.* New York: Brunner/Mazel Inc.

Ryan, R.M., Mims, V., & Koestner, R. (1983). Relation of reward contingency and interpersonal context to intrinsic motivation: A review and test using cognitive evaluation theory. *Journal of Personality and Social Psychology, 45,* 736-750.

Sattler, J.M. (2002). *Assessment of children: Behavioral and clinical applications* (4th ed.). San Diego, CA: Jerome M. Satter, Publisher, Inc.

Wiener, J.M., Jaffe, S.L., Goldstein, G.A., & Justice, L.R. (1996). Historical overview of childhood and adolescent psychopharmacology. In J.M. Wiener (Ed.) *Diagnosis and psychopharmacology of childhood and adolescent disorders* (pp. 3-69). New York: John Wiley & Sons, Inc.

APPENDIX A
Behavior Observation Form

BEHAVIORAL OBSERVATION SHEET

Today's Date: _____ **Observer:** _____

Observation Start Time: _____ **Stop Time:** _____

Participant Identification: _____ **Grade:** _____

Teacher Name: _____ **Activity:** _____

Coding: X = On-task   O = Off-task

Rater Instructions: Complete the information section. During the first 10 seconds of each half-minute, code an X if the participant demonstrates on-task behavior and an O if the participant demonstrates off-task behavior for the interval. On-task behavior: (a) the student is seated at his or her desk or appropriate work-place; (b) the student's hands are manipulating only items necessary for the on-going teacher-specified activity; (c) the student's head is oriented toward the direction dictated by the teacher-specified activity.

One-to-one interaction occurred: yes _____   no _____

Rater Comments:

APPENDIX B
Teacher Training Session

1. Welcome and appreciation for participating

2. Purpose of the study

   This study will investigate the effectiveness of praise, used as a directive, on the classroom attention of elementary school students, that you identify as having a low level of attention. Specifically, we are examining: Does praise, used as a directive, increase attention to task?

3. Definition of Terms

   A. Participant:
      A student whose level of inattention interferes with his or her academic progress
      He or she achieves above average scores on a rating scale measuring classroom attention
      Students currently or historically receiving Special Education services are excluded.

   B. On-task behavior:
      The student is seated at his or her desk or appropriate work-place
      The student's hands are manipulating only items necessary for the activity
      The student's head is oriented toward the direction dictated by the activity

   C. Praise:
      Praise is a descriptive statement, given to the student by you in regards to the student's on-task behavior. Its purpose is to direct the student's attention to genuine progress or accomplishment and to set a goal for future performance. As such, effective praise is descriptive as opposed to judgmental and is given in a genuine manner.

      It includes:
         Use of the student's name
         A statement of appreciation
         A specific description of the behavior being praised
         Consideration of a future goal

      During the treatment conditions of this study, praise will be given individually to the student, by the teacher, at the close of the targeted academic period. The teacher will reiterate the statement preceding the next day's reading lesson.

4. Mechanics of the study

   Referral criterion, parent permission, behavior rating scale, noting an appropriate on-task behavior, administration of praise

5. Sample scripts

   Joey, when I was talking about the new word during reading yesterday you kept your eyes on your book or me. I appreciate how hard you were trying to see the new word in your book. I'd like to see you do that again today.

   Wow, Miranda, what a wonderful job you did remembering to sit in your seat during reading yesterday. Even though you were excited, you remembered and sat down. I appreciate your good work because it helps all the children concentrate on our work when we all remember to stay in our seats. I can't wait to see you do that again today.

   Congratulations, Johnny, although your fingers wanted to touch Jimmy's work during reading yesterday, you remembered to bring your hands back to yourself. I appreciate it when you remember to keep your hands on your own papers because it is respectful to your classmates. I'll bet you can remember to tell your hands to remain on your own desk even better today.

   Way to go, Kimmy. Thank you for listening quietly while Matt read out loud in reading yesterday. It makes people feel special when you listen to them, and I appreciate your helping me feel special by listening to Matt read. It'll be fun to see how you listen today.

6. Practice vignettes

APPENDIX C
Praise Record Form

Delayed Praise Treatment I

Praise Statement includes:

Use of the student's name
A statement of appreciation
A specific description of the behavior being praised
Consideration of a future goal

Day 4, praise statement to use on day 5

Day 5, praise statement to use on day 6

Day 6, praise statement to use on day 7

Day 7, praise statement to use on day 8

APPENDIX D
Delayed Praise Daily Schedule

Day 1: No changes in your teaching interaction

Day 2: No changes in your teaching interaction

Day 3: No changes in your teaching interaction

Day 4: Observe for an on-task behavior you would like to reinforce tomorrow. Following the lesson, praise the behavior and write the praise statement that you will use tomorrow.

Day 5: Prior to the instructional activity, praise the student for yesterday's on-task behavior. During the activity observe for an appropriate on-task behavior. Following the lesson, praise today's behavior and write the statement for tomorrow's instructional activity.

Day 6: Prior to the instructional activity, praise the student for yesterday's on-task behavior. During the activity observe for an appropriate on-task behavior. Following the lesson, praise today's behavior and write the statement for tomorrow's instructional activity.

Day 7: Prior to the instructional activity, praise the student for yesterday's on-task behavior. During the activity observe for an appropriate on-task behavior. Following the lesson, praise today's behavior and write the statement for tomorrow's instructional activity.

Day 8: Prior to the instructional activity praise the student for yesterday's on-task behavior.

Day 9: Baseline condition. Do not use delayed praise statement before the instructional activity.

Day 10: Baseline condition. Do not use delayed praise statement.

Day 11: Baseline condition. Do not use delayed praise statement.

Day 12: Baseline condition. Do not use delayed praise statement before the instructional activity. During the activity observe for an appropriate on-task behavior. Following the lesson, praise the behavior and write the statement that you will use tomorrow.

Day 13: Prior to the instructional activity, praise the student for yesterday's on-task behavior. During the activity observe for an appropriate on-task behavior. Following the lesson, praise the behavior and write the statement that you will use tomorrow.

Day 14: Prior to the instructional activity, praise the student for yesterday's on-task behavior. During the activity observe for an appropriate on-task behavior. Following the lesson, praise the behavior and write the statement that you will use tomorrow.

Day 15: Prior to the instructional activity, praise the student for yesterday's on-task behavior. During the activity observe for an appropriate on-task behavior. Following the lesson, praise the behavior and write the statement that you will use tomorrow.

Day 16: Prior to the instructional activity, praise the student for yesterday's on-task behavior.

Decreasing Transition Times in a Second Grade Classroom: Scientific Support for the Timely Transitions Game

Jamie L. Yarbrough
Christopher H. Skinner
Young Ju Lee

University of Tennessee

Cathy Lemmons

Knox County School System

SUMMARY. Campbell and Skinner used an A-B design to evaluate the effects of the Timely Transitions Game (TTG) on room-to-room transitions in a sixth-grade classroom. The TTG incorporated explicit timing, publicly posted feedback, and an interdependent group contingency with randomly selected transitions and criteria. The purpose of the current study was to use scientific procedures including (a) an experimental design, (b) interobserver agreement data, (c) treatment integrity data, and

Address correspondence to: Christopher H. Skinner, PhD, The University of Tennessee, College of EHHS, Claxton Complex A-518, Knoxville, TN 37996-3452 (E-mail: cskinne1@utk.edu).

[Haworth co-indexing entry note]: "Decreasing Transition Times in a Second Grade Classroom: Scientific Support for the Timely Transitions Game." Yarbrough et al. Co-published simultaneously in *Journal of Applied School Psychology* (The Haworth Press, Inc.) Vol. 20, No. 2, 2004, pp. 85-107; and: *Single-Subject Designs for School Psychologists* (ed: Christopher H. Skinner) The Haworth Press, Inc., 2004, pp. 85-107. Single or multiple copies of this article are available for a fee from The Haworth Document Delivery Service [1-800-HAWORTH, 9:00 a.m. - 5:00 p.m. (EST). E-mail address: docdelivery@haworthpress.com].

Digital Object Identifier: 10.1300/J008v20n02_06   *85*

(d) procedural integrity data to validate the efficacy of a modified TTG on after lunch hallway-to-classroom transitions in an intact second-grade classroom. Across-phase comparisons of transition times revealed clear experimental control and suggest that the TTG caused decreases in transition times. Discussion focuses on empirical case studies, validating interventions, and using interdependent group reinforcement in a classroom setting. *[Article copies available for a fee from The Haworth Document Delivery Service: 1-800-HAWORTH. E-mail address: <docdelivery@haworthpress.com> Website: <http://www.HaworthPress.com>* © *2004 by The Haworth Press, Inc. All rights reserved.]*

KEYWORDS. Withdrawal design, interdependent group contingency, Timely Transitions Game, experimental control, explicit timing

In response to a sixth-grade teacher's request for assistance in reducing room-to-room transition times, Campbell and Skinner developed and evaluated the Timely Transitions Game (TTG). The researchers developed the TTG by combining three empirically validated intervention procedures: (a) interdependent group-oriented contingencies with randomly selected target behaviors and criteria, (b) explicit timing procedures, and (c) publicly posted group feedback.

GROUP CONTINGENCIES

Group-oriented contingencies have been found to be effective and efficient procedures for managing students' classroom behavior (Gresham & Gresham, 1982; Skinner, Skinner, & Sterling-Turner, 2002). In their meta-analysis, Stage and Quiroz (1997) found that group-oriented contingencies were the most effective procedure (i.e., largest effect size) for reducing inappropriate classroom behavior. Additionally, interdependent group-oriented contingencies, where groups of students are reinforced on an all-or-none basis contingent upon some group criteria (e.g., class average), are incorporated into several interventions that have been shown to enhance academic achievement and skill development including *The Academic Behavior Game* (Popkin & Skinner, 2003), *Classwide Peer Tutoring* (Greenwood, Delquadri, & Carta, 1997), and various cooperative learning interventions (Slavin, 1987).

While interdependent group contingencies have been shown to be effective, these procedures can also occasion some negative side effects including (a) students attempting to encourage peers to help the group meet their goal with inappropriate behaviors (e.g., threatening peers with social or physical aggression), (b) individual students sabotaging the group's success, and (c) large groups of students becoming discouraged when they judge that the group can no longer meet their goals (Lew, Mesch, Johnson, & Johnson, 1986; Romeo, 1998; Skinner, Cashwell, & Dunn, 1996). Randomly selecting rewards from an established pool of rewards may reduce sabotage, provided that for each student the pool of rewards contains at least one high quality reinforcer (Moore, Waguespack, Wickstrom, Witt, & Gaydos, 1994; Skinner et al., 1996). Employing randomly selected, unknown, or indiscriminable criteria for earning access to group rewards may (a) encourage students to do their best, (b) prevent students from giving up because they feel that the group cannot meet the group oriented criteria, (c) reduce peer pressure on an individual student, and (d) increase the probability of students maintaining desired behaviors after the contingency program is withdrawn (Freeland & Noell, 1999; Freeland & Noell, 2002; Kelshaw-Levering, Sterling-Turner, Henry, & Skinner, 2000; Gresham & Gresham, 1982; Popkin & Skinner, 2003; Skinner, Williams, & Neddenriep, in press; Theodore, Bray, Kehle, & Jenson, 2001).

Explicit Timing and Publicly Posted Feedback

Van Houten and Thompson (1976) showed that setting time limits and explicitly or overtly timing students (e.g., starting a stopwatch in front of students) causes them to increase their academic task completion rates. Subsequent studies showed that such procedures improved students' speed of responding across students, academic tasks, and settings, and were effective when teachers or others employed the explicit timing procedures (Derr & Shapiro, 1989; Derr-Minneci & Shapiro, 1992; Evans, Skinner, Henington, Sims, & McDaniel, 2002; Rhymer, Henington, Skinner, & Looby, 1999; Rhymer, Skinner, Henington, D'Reaux, & Sims, 1998; Rhymer, Skinner, Jackson, McNeill, Smith, & Jackson, 2002).

Scientific studies have shown that explicit timing procedures are effective across students, target behaviors, and settings. Van Houten, Hill, and Parsons (1975) used component analysis procedures to determine if adding publicly posted feedback to explicit timing procedures enhances the efficacy of explicit timing procedures. Results showed that explicit timing and publicly posted feedback caused greater increases in speed of academic responding than merely explicit timing.

Applied scientific studies have shown that interdependent-group oriented contingencies also can be used to alter class-wide responding. Researchers also have shown that explicit timing procedures enhance speed of responding and that even greater increases in speed of responding are obtained when explicit timing is combined with publicly posted feedback. Campbell and Skinner combined these three empirically validated procedures to develop the TTG, an intervention designed to make transitions speedier.

Timely Transitions Game

Campbell and Skinner's TTG included interdependent contingencies with randomly selected criteria and target behaviors, explicit timing, and publicly posted feedback. Specifically, after baseline, students' transition rules were developed and posted in the classroom. Students then were provided direct instruction with respect to transitions. Rules were reviewed, students practiced transitions, and feedback was provided regarding appropriate and inappropriate transition behaviors during these practice transitions. Next, the class was told that they would earn a group reinforcer if their transition times were equal to or less than a randomly drawn criterion. Daily, the teacher explicitly timed five room-to-room transitions. During these transitions, she stopped the class in the hallway and started the stopwatch when any student misbehaved. After students ceased breaking transition rules, the teacher stopped the stopwatch and instructed the class to continue transitioning.

After each of the five daily transitions, the teacher publicly posted the students' transition time by writing the transition times on a chart posted in the front of the classroom. Finally, the teacher implemented an interdependent group contingency. At the end of the school day, the teacher randomly selected a transition criterion (number of seconds) and a target transition (from the five daily transitions). If the randomly selected transition was completed in fewer seconds than the randomly selected criterion, a letter was placed on the chart. The letters spelled out a group reward (e.g., P-A-R-T-Y) that all class members would receive when all the letters were earned.

Results of Campbell and Skinner's empirical case study showed that transition times decreased immediately after the intervention was implemented and remained much briefer than baseline. After the TTG was implemented, weekly transition times were reduced by approximately 2 hours.

Limitation of Previous Research

Campbell and Skinner's data show *immediate, large*, and *sustained* reductions in transition times after the TTG was implemented. From an applied perspective, these results are impressive. However, several limitations associated with Campbell and Skinner's methods hindered their ability to determine if the TTG caused the reduction in transition times. Campbell and Skinner used an empirical case study as opposed to an experimental design. While case studies have applied value, they do not control for threats to internal validity (Skinner, Waterson, Bryant, Bryant, Collins, Hill, Tipton, Ragsdale, & Fox, 2002). For example, in the Campbell and Skinner study it is possible that transition times may have been reduced because different behavior management procedures were instituted in the classroom that enhanced student pre-transition behavior. Previous research on setting events or establishing operations (McGill, 1999; Michael, 1993; Smith & Iwata, 1997) suggests that such changes could have reduced transition times. If these behavior management procedures were implemented concurrently with the TTG, then reductions in transition times may have not caused the changes. This threat to internal validity is typically referred to as history (Campbell & Stanley, 1966).

The apparent solution to this issue would be to investigate (e.g., interview teachers, collect direct observation data) and determine if such changes in behavior management procedures were instituted. However, such procedures cannot be used to control for history threats in applied research, as we have not, and never will have identified all the variables or environmental events that could affect behavior. If we ever do reach this point, then there will be little or no need to conduct theoretical research on human behavior, and sciences like psychology and sociology would be less relevant.

If we cannot identify all of these other variables that may have influenced behavior (i.e., history threats), then it is impossible to directly assess such events in order to rule them out as causal variables. Thus, Campbell and Skinner's empirical case study (e.g., A-B) design did not allow them to determine if the intervention caused the reduction in transition times.

Another limitation of Campbell and Skinner's study is related to the data that was used to evaluate the effects of the intervention. Campbell and Skinner's case study appears to have more scientific merit than other case study methodologies in which researchers interpret non-empirical data based on some theory (e.g., psychoanalytic case studies or qualitative studies). However, inclusion of empirical data does not mean that scientific procedures were followed. Because Campbell and Skinner did not collect interobserver agreement data, the quality of their empirical data is suspect, just as the quality of subjective interpretations of non-empirical data (e.g., dream interpretation) is suspect.

Because Campbell and Skinner did not assess for changes in observer recording behavior (e.g., reactivity, observer drift), changes in student transition time may have been caused by inconsistent data collection procedures (Hersen & Barlow, 1982; Johnson & Bolstad, 1973). For example, the teacher may have systematically changed her timing procedures (e.g., criteria for starting and stopping the stopwatch) after the intervention was implemented.

In the Campbell and Skinner study, the quality of the dependent variable was never evaluated. However, researchers did collect treatment integrity data to attempt to evaluate the quality of the independent variable. These data were collected by the experimenter who looked at the poster board at the end of the day to determine if the teacher (a) recorded transition times, (b) recorded a randomly selected criteria, (c) recorded a randomly selected transition, (d) publicly posted a letter when the recorded randomly selected transition met the recorded randomly selected criterion or (e) did not post a letter when the recorded randomly selected transition did not meet the recorded randomly selected criterion. While these treatment integrity data suggest that the teacher generally carried out the intervention with integrity, it is possible that she did not. For example, there were no data to determine if she implemented the timing procedures consistently and as described. Additionally, there are no data to show that she randomly selected target behaviors and criteria. Having an independent observer directly observe and record the treatment implementation behaviors would have provided a much stronger indication that the treatment was implemented with integrity.

Purpose of the Current Study

The current experiment was designed to extend the research on the TTG in several ways. First, a multi-phase withdrawal design was used so that researchers could provide for repeated demonstration of experimental control. Such procedures allowed researchers to control for extraneous variables (e.g., history) that may have contaminated the previous study. Second, interobserver agreement, treatment integrity, and procedural integrity data were collected using direct observation to control for threats to internal validity associated with inconsistent assessment procedure, intervention procedures, and experimental procedures (i.e., integrity associated with the no-treatment condition).

In addition to enhancing the internal validity of Campbell and Skinner's case study, external validity was enhanced by conducting the study in a second-grade urban classroom of African-American students. Finally, student and teacher acceptability was assessed. While these data provide little information related to experimental control, they do provide information with respect to application of the intervention and generalizability to other classrooms. Specifically, if teachers find intervention procedures acceptable, they may be more likely to choose to implement those procedures in their classrooms (Elliott, 1988; Zins & Ponti, 1990). Additionally, if students find interventions acceptable, they may be more cooperative and responsive (Turco & Elliott, 1990).

METHOD

Participants and Setting

Participants were 15 African-American students (three girls and 12 boys) from an intact second-grade classroom in an urban Southeastern public school. The teacher was a Caucasian woman with 17 years of teaching experience. The teacher's assistant was an African-American woman with four years of experience. Two school psychology graduate students collected data and worked with the classroom teacher to implement the procedures.

The teacher requested assistance from the researchers to address problems with the class's *after lunch* transitions. She indicated that this transition was taking an especially long time because after entering the classroom the students engaged in time-consuming misbehaviors such as jumping, yelling, running, dancing, laughing, hitting, pushing, and screaming. The teacher indicated that the time required for calming the students reduced the time available for instruction and academic work following lunch.

The classroom contained 15 student desks, arranged in a U-shape around the blackboard. The teacher's desk and a reading table were at the back of the room. As the students entered the room, the teacher's desk and table were immediately to the left, blackboard to the front, and student desks in-between. A large open space in the middle of the desks contained hanging artwork. After returning from the cafeteria, the students typically congregated in this open space in the middle of their classroom, often displaying inappropriate behaviors.

The teaching assistant was responsible for supervising the children in the lunchroom and during the transition back to the classroom after lunch. Typically, the students would line up against the wall outside of the classroom, and the teaching assistant would give the teacher a behavior report before the students were allowed into the classroom. After this was finished, the students would run into the classroom and misbehave while the teacher and teaching assistant continued to talk.

Materials

A digital stopwatch was used to measure transition times. A shoebox with a hole in the top was used to store the cards with transition times printed on them. The shoebox was covered with decorative wrapping paper. Researchers constructed 13 transition time cards using colored markers and construction paper. Colorful letters were also constructed with construction paper and laminated. Additional materials included teacher purchased rewards (e.g., popcorn) or rented rewards (i.e., movies).

Teacher and students' perceptions of the intervention were assessed. The teacher completed the Behavior Intervention Rating Scale (Von Brock & Elliott, 1987), which consists of 24 questions with Likert scale responses ranging from 1 (Strongly Disagree) to 6 (Strongly Agree). Research on the BIRS suggests it has adequate psychometric properties (Von Brock & Elliott, 1987).

Additionally, the researchers modified the Children's Intervention Rating Scale (Witt & Elliott, 1985). Specifically, researchers selected only six questions to measure student acceptability of the intervention. This measure was administered to the entire class. The students were given the form (see Table 1), and a researcher read questions aloud and the students responded by raising their hands to indicate a *yes*, *no*, or *maybe* response. Although the CIRP appears to have adequate psychometric properties (Turco & Elliott, 1986), this measure was modified and administered in this manner (students raising their hand) because the students' teacher reported that many of her second-grade students would not be able to read and understand all of the items and, therefore, would be unable to provide meaningful or valid responses if asked to complete the form independently.

Procedures

At the time that the study began, the teacher reported that she had not employed any systematic procedures designed to improve the students' behavior when returning from lunch. While there were not any consis-

TABLE 1. Student Acceptability Items with the Number of Students Responding *Yes*, *Maybe*, and *No* in Brackets.

This game helped my classmates stay out of trouble	Yes (15)	Maybe (0)	No (0)
This game was fair	Yes (14)	Maybe (0)	No (1)
This game was fun	Yes (14)	Maybe (0)	No (1)
This game helped me stay out of trouble	Yes (14)	Maybe (0)	No (1)
Other teachers should use this game	Yes (12)	Maybe (1)	No (2)
This game would work at other times of the day	Yes (7)	Maybe (0)	No (8)

tent consequences for misbehavior during the transition, a response cost system was used to address inappropriate behavior throughout the school day. Specifically, each student began the day with three *tickets*. The tickets were worth 10 minutes of playtime each day, for a total of 30 minutes. When a student misbehaved, the teacher could remove a ticket at her discretion. This independent group-oriented response cost system was used in all of the second-grade classrooms at the school. This particular teacher had modified her ticket system so that her students had the opportunity to earn back lost tickets. Again, students earned tickets back at the teacher's discretion. Although this system was the primary structured source of consequences for misbehavior, the teacher reported that she reserved taking tickets for serious misbehaviors (e.g., fighting). Consequently, the children often did not lose tickets for the misbehaviors they displayed when returning from lunch.

The majority of instructional activities took place in the morning. The teacher noted that the children were usually well-behaved and attentive to her instructions until they returned from lunch. After lunch, they typically spent 45 minutes studying mathematics and 45 minutes doing a quiet activity, such as writing in journals. A 30-minute recess divided these academic periods. Although there were several other transitions during the day, the teacher indicated that the only time when there was a serious problem was after lunch.

Design. A withdrawal design was used to evaluate the effectiveness of the TTG. This design is superior to most single-subject or group designs because it provides for repeated demonstrations of within-subject or within-group functional relations (Hersen & Barlow, 1982). In the current study, a six phase withdrawal design (i.e., A-B-A-B-A-B phases) was used. A-phases represent baseline (initial A-phase) or withdrawal (the second and third A-phases) conditions and B-phases represented intervention (i.e., TTG) conditions. These six phases allowed for five demonstrations of experimental control. Comparisons of B-phase data with previous adjacent A-phase data allowed for three demonstrations that the TTG decreased transition times. Comparing the withdrawal phase data (i.e., second and third A-phases) to previous adjacent intervention or B-phase data, allowed for two additional evaluations of experimental control. Specifically, if transition times increased after the intervention was withdrawn (i.e., the data showed a reversal or return to previous baseline levels), then these comparisons would provide additional evidence that the intervention caused the change in transition times.

Data Collection Procedures. During all phases, the researchers used direct observation procedures to record the amount of time that it took the students to enter the room and sit quietly at their desks. Specifically, each day, one or two researchers (two researchers when interobserver agreement was collected), entered the classroom before the students returned from lunch and sat in the back of the room. Researchers covertly started a stopwatch (i.e., the stopwatch was kept out of view by holding it behind data-recording sheets) when the first student crossed the threshold. When all students were quietly seated in their assigned desks for 5 seconds the researcher(s) stopped the stopwatch and recorded the number of seconds required for the transition.

Experimental Phases. During the baseline phase (first A-Phase), the researchers merely collected transition time data. After the initial 3 days of baseline, the teacher reviewed the baseline data and selected criteria that would constitute an acceptable transition time. These criteria ranged from 40 seconds to 100 seconds in 5-second increments. Next, a variation of the TTG was implemented.

The teacher explained the procedures associated with the TTG to the students before they left for lunch and then reminded them of the procedures when they returned from lunch, before they were instructed to enter the classroom. Specifically, the teacher showed the class a stopwatch and told the class she would start the stopwatch when the first student entered the room after returning from lunch. She informed them that the watch would run until everyone was quietly seated in their desk (no audible sounds for 5 seconds), at which point she would stop the stopwatch and write the transition time on the chalkboard.

She then explained that she would randomly select (draw) a transition time card out of the box at the end of the day and that class would earn a letter if their time beat the time drawn from the box. She then showed the students a couple of criterion time cards and listed the 13 times on the blackboard. Times ranged from 40 seconds to 100 seconds in 5-second increments. To make the times clear to the students, times over 1 minute were written on the cards and on the blackboard in minutes and seconds. Thus, 100 seconds was written as 1 minute and 40 seconds.

Next the teacher explained the group reward procedure. She told the students that when they earned all the letters in the word party, *P-A-R-T-Y*, that they would have a party the next school day during which everyone could eat candy and drink soft drinks. Next, she showed the class the letters and explained that they would be taped to the top of the blackboard each day they met the randomly selected transition criterion. The teacher answered students' questions and then they transitioned to lunch under the assistant teacher's supervision.

After returning from lunch, the TTG was implemented. While the students were in the hallway, the teacher reminded them of the TTG and started the stopwatch as the first student in line entered the room. When all the students were seated and quiet for 5 seconds, she stopped the stopwatch in plain view of the students and recorded their transition time on the blackboard. Similar procedures were used across all intervention sessions.

The first intervention phase lasted 8 days. After that, a 3-day withdrawal phase was implemented. During this phase, conditions returned to baseline conditions (i.e., data was collected using covert timing, no letters were provided, and transition times were not posted), and students were told that they were not playing the game.

During the second intervention phase, students earned letters spelling the word *M-O-V-I-E*, and were allowed to watch a movie when all the letters were earned. This phase only took 5 days as students earned a letter each day. After a brief 1-day withdrawal, during which students were once again told that they were not playing the game, a third intervention phase was implemented during which the students earned *P-O-P-C-O-R-N*.

Following this intervention phase, the experimenters stopped collecting data. However, the teacher continued to implement the program with a couple of alterations. First, she altered the program by removing some of the longer interval criterion slips and replacing them with criterion slips with short intervals. Second, she altered the reinforcers. In the next phase, the students earned *C-U-P-C-A-K-E-S*. This was chosen because a student volunteered to bring in cupcakes, thus saving teacher time and teacher resources. Additionally, the number of letters needed to earn the reward increased to seven. Thus, reinforcement rate may have been faded and the effort required to earn the reward was increased. Research suggests that both of these procedures enhance maintenance of behavior change after interventions are withdrawn (see Skinner, Williams, & Neddenriep, in press).

Interobserver Agreement, Treatment Integrity, and Procedural Integrity

During this study, the teacher and one of two researchers independently measured and recorded transition times each day. The transition times recorded by the researchers served as the dependent variable. Additionally, another researcher independently timed and recorded transition time data on 34% of all transitions. Recorded transition times across the two researchers differed by no more than 2 seconds across observers. Correlations between the two observers were strong, $r > .99$.

Additionally, on 7 of the 21 intervention days, both independent observers collected treatment integrity data. On each day, treatment integrity data was 100% as the independent observer recorded the teacher (a) starting the stopwatch when the first student entered the room, (b) stopping the stopwatch after the students were in their seat and quiet for approximately 5 seconds, (c) writing the transition times on the board, (d) randomly selecting a criterion transition time, (e) reading the randomly selected time to the class, and (f) taping the appropriate letter to the blackboard if they beat their time or not awarding a letter when the class did not meet the randomly selected transition time. Both researchers collected this data independently. Interobserver agreement for treatment integrity was 100%.

Procedural integrity data was collected for one baseline session and three of the four withdrawal sessions. During the three withdrawal sessions, both researchers observed the teacher inform the students that they were not playing the game prior to leaving from lunch. During all four no-treatment sessions that procedural integrity data was collected both observers' data showed that the teacher did not perform any of the TTG behaviors (see items a-f on the treatment integrity checklist described in the previous paragraph) during any of the sessions. Again, both researchers collected this data independently and interobserver agreement for procedural integrity during baseline was 100%.

RESULTS

Figure 1 displays transition time data across phases. During the initial 3-day baseline phase, each transition time exceeded 2.5 minutes. The average transition time during this phase was 178 seconds (range 159 to 215). Following the implementation of the TTG, transition times showed an immediate decrease. Although the data from this phase shows some variability (transition times ranged from 35 seconds to 113 seconds), no transition exceeded 2 minutes, and the average transition time was 59 seconds. The first intervention phase lasted 8 days. On 3 of those days, the class's transition time was not sufficient to meet the criterion that was randomly selected at the end of the school day.

After the group earned their first award, the TTG game was withdrawn. During the first withdrawal phase (i.e., second A-phase), before the class transitioned to lunch the teacher informed the students that they were not playing the game. Figure 1 shows that withdrawing the TTG had little immediate effect on transition time (i.e., little difference between baseline and intervention on the first day the intervention was implemented). However, after this first day, transition times increased dramatically, returning to baseline levels (i.e., initial A-phase levels).

Figure 1 shows that reintroduction of the TTG (i.e., second B-phase) resulted in an immediate reduction in transition times. Additionally, transition times during this phase were much more stable than during the first intervention phase (range of 33-55 seconds). The class met the randomly selected criteria each day during this phase.

FIGURE 1. Daily Transition Times Across A Phases (i.e., Baseline and Withdraw Phases) and B Phases (i.e., Timely Transitions Game Phases).

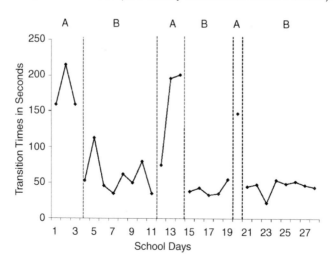

During the second withdrawal phase (i.e., third A-phase which lasted only 1 day), the transition time increased immediately to 186 seconds. During the final 8-day intervention phase (i.e., final B-phase), transition times returned to previous intervention phase levels. Throughout this phase, no transitions exceeded 52 seconds and the class met the randomly selected criteria each day.

When comparisons across the five adjacent phases are made, Figure 1 shows clear changes in transition times as the treatment was applied and withdrawn. With the exception of the first day of the initial withdrawal phase, across phase comparisons show immediate changes in transition times and no overlapping data points across adjacent phases. Thus, the current experiment provides five demonstrations of experimental control.

Student Acceptability

On the second to last day of the final intervention phase, one experimenter read questions from the modified Children's Intervention Rating Profile (CIRP) aloud, and the students raised their hands to indicate their answers. The experimenter answered students' questions about items and response options (i.e., yes, no, or maybe) prior to asking them to raise their hands. Table 1 provides the questions and summarizes their responses. These data show that all students reported that the TTG helped their classmates stay out of trouble. All but one student reported the game was fair, fun, and helped him or her stay out of trouble. Additionally, 80% reported that other teachers should use this game. These data suggest that the students found the game acceptable (fun, fair, and helpful). However, Table 1 shows that less than 50% (i.e., 7/15) reported that the TTG should be used at other times of the day. Perhaps responses to this item were not measuring acceptability. Recall that the teacher reported that the class typically had efficient transitions at all other times during the school day. Thus, she only wanted to target the after lunch transition. Thus, student responses to this item may reflect some students' opinion that the TTG was not needed for other transitions.

Teacher Acceptability

The teacher filled out the Behavior Intervention Rating Scale (BIRS), which consists of 24 questions with Likert scale responses ranging from 1 (*Strongly Disagree*) to 6 (*Strongly Agree*). Across all items the teacher's average score was 5.333. Of those questions, she rated 17 of them as strongly agree (i.e., response of 6) and six questions as agree (i.e., response of 5) indicating strong levels of acceptability. However, the teacher responded *disagree* (i.e., 2) to one question–"The child's behavior will remain at an improved level even after the intervention is discontinued." This response was expected as the withdrawal phases showed that the children's behavior did not remain improved after the intervention was withdrawn.

Post Intervention Procedures

After the researchers discontinued collecting transition data, the teacher continued to run the intervention. However, she began to implement a procedure designed to fade the frequency of reinforcement. Specifically, she altered the transition time criteria pool by eliminating all times over 1 minute and replacing those times with briefer times. Additionally, she continued to use rewards that were composed of longer and longer letters.

DISCUSSION

From Practice to Research

Within-Group Replication of Effects. Campbell and Skinner used an A-B design to evaluate the effects of the TTG on room-to-room transitions in a sixth-grade classroom. The current experiment extends this research in several ways. In the current study, researchers employed a withdrawal design with six separate phases. This design allowed for five within-group demonstrations of experimental control. Changes in transition times occurred after phase changes, in the predicted direction, and tended to be maintained throughout each phase. Thus, these results provide for five across-phase demonstrations of experimental control. Three of these demonstrations showed a decrease in transition times across the TTG treatment phases (B-phases) and the preceding adjacent no treatment phases (A-phases). These adjacent A-B comparisons demonstrate experimental control. The two comparisons across B-phases (TTG phases) and the following A-phases (withdrawal phases) provide two additional demonstrations of experimental control as the students' transition times immediately increased after the treatment was withdrawn, quickly returning to baseline (initial A-phase) levels.

Interobserver Agreement. In the Campbell and Skinner study, the teacher's timing data served as the primary dependent variable and there were no interobserver agreement checks. Because no data were collected to evaluate the quality or consistency of these data collection procedures, it is possible that these data were compromised. For example, expectancy effects or the teacher's desire for students to earn reinforcement may have caused the teacher to inadvertently alter her timing procedures to increase the probability of students meeting the criteria during the intervention phase. In the current study, interobserver agreement data were collected and suggest that data were collected consistently, thus providing evidence that inconsistent data collection procedures (e.g., observer drift, instrumentation) did not account for the systematic changes in transition times depicted in Figure 1.

Treatment Integrity. Campbell and Skinner collected treatment integrity data by checking the poster where data were recorded. While these observations of permanent products provided some indication of integrity, they did not allow the researchers to determine if the teacher actually performed each of these behaviors at the appropriate time or with integrity. In the current study, a researcher collected treatment integrity data each day that the treatment was implemented. These direct observation data provide for a more accurate assessment of integrity and suggest that the intervention was implemented with integrity 100% of the session.

Additionally, in the current study another independent observer used direct observation procedures to collect integrity data on 34% of the intervention sessions. This allowed researchers to calculate interobserver agreement data on integrity. While this is not typically done, the rationale for requiring interobserver agreement on the dependent variable can clearly be applied to the independent variable. In the current study, the treatment integrity data (B-phases) and the agreement between two independent observers provide clear support for the assertion that the treatment was implemented as designed (Noell & Witt, 1998).

Procedural Integrity. Researchers have argued for the need to collect treatment integrity data (Gresham, 1989; Witt, Gresham, & Noell, 1996). However, when experimental designs are used with other conditions or phases, from an experimental or science-based perspective, it is also critical to show that these phases or conditions were implemented with integrity. In the current study, we used the term *procedural integrity* when referring to teacher behavior during baseline and withdrawal phases. Specifically, we collected these data to ensure that the teacher did not implement any of the intervention procedures during the no-treatment sessions (i.e., baseline and withdrawal phases). Additionally, we verified these data by having another observer independently record these data on four of seven sessions. These data support the assertion that the teacher did not implement treatment procedures during the no-treatment conditions.

Summary of Enhanced Experimental Procedures. Treatment and procedural integrity data suggest that inconsistent intervention implementation did not contaminate the results. However, these data alone do not indicate that the intervention caused the change because such procedures cannot be used to collect data on all possible events outside of the experiments' control that may have caused the change (i.e., history effects). Instead, the design (withdrawal design) that allowed for five within-group replications of experimental effects controlled for these other confounding variables. After all, what is the probability that some other event (i.e., history effect) caused the changes in the opposite direction at five specific times and only at those times?

Had experimental data shown no change in transition times across phases, procedural integrity data would have been critical. In this situation, if treatment integrity (TTG or B-phase data) showed that the intervention had not been implemented as planned, then these data could prevent researchers from concluding that the intervention was ineffective, when, in fact, intervention effects were never actually evaluated because the treatment was not implemented with integrity.

In the current study, researchers also collected procedural integrity data during withdrawal phases. These data suggest that the teacher did withdraw all elements of the TTG during these phases. For drawing cause-and-effect conclusions, these data may be as critical as treatment integrity data. For example, in the current study, suppose that transition times did not increase or return to initial baseline levels during either withdrawal phase. If this occurred, then there would be only one across phase comparison (initial A-B) suggesting experimental control, and our data look like and be no more useful than the data from Campbell and Skinner's A-B design. Therefore, we would not have been able to rule out the possibility that some other event that occurred at approximately the same time as the intervention (i.e., history) caused the change in transition times.

Campbell and Skinner's empirical case study suggested that the TTG may have reduced transition time in an intact sixth-grade classroom. However, Campbell and Skinner provided only one demonstration of experimental control. The current study does more than suggest that the TTG caused changes in students' behavior. With five within-group replications of experimental control, the current study rules out other causal variables (threats to internal validity) that may have accounted for the changes. Additionally, in the current study we collected data which suggests that inconsistent (a) data collection procedures (i.e., interobserver agreement), (b) treatment implementations procedures (i.e., treatment integrity), and (c) withdrawal procedures (i.e., procedural integrity data collected during no-treatment sessions) did not account for these reported changes in transition times.

Future Research

The current intervention was designed to be time efficient, cost effective, and easy to implement. Though the intervention was performed daily over a 7-week period, it typically took less than 5 minutes to implement. Given these characteristics of the intervention, it is not surprising that both the teacher and her students found the TTG acceptable. Student responses to the acceptability questionnaire suggest that they found the intervention acceptable. Additional evidence was observed during the withdrawal phases. On the first day of the first withdrawal phase, when the students saw the researchers, they quickly sat in their desks and asked what their time for the day was. After they were reminded that they were not playing the game anymore, several students complained and the following transition times increased dramatically. During the second withdrawal phase, upon seeing the researchers, the students began to suggest words that they could work on to earn. These actions are clear indicators of the popularity or acceptability of the intervention.

After the popcorn was earned, the researchers encouraged the teacher to continue with the game, and also work on fading the procedure. The fading procedure selected was to lengthen the number of letters students were required to earn before receiving reinforcers. The teacher solicited input from students and selected C-U-P-C-A-K-E-S as the next reinforcer. Not only did this include more letters, but also, a student volunteered to bring in the cupcakes after they won. For the remainder of the school year (approximately 3 weeks after the students earned cupcakes), the teacher continued to use the TTG in this fashion. The teacher's responses to the acceptability questionnaire suggest that she found the intervention acceptable. The teacher's decision to continue this intervention after the research was completed provides equally, if not more, compelling evidence that she found it acceptable. In an unstructured interview at the end of the year, the teacher reported that the

TTG required little time and effort and improved her emotional state during the afternoon as she no longer had to prompt, pester, or yell at the children to get them settled after lunch. Additionally, the teacher reported that she shared this intervention with other teachers at her school.

The current study extended previous research by showing that the TTG was effective in reducing transition times in a second-grade classroom of African-American students. Additionally, empirical and non-empirical acceptability data suggest that both the teacher and students found the intervention to be effective. Therefore, future researchers should conduct additional type II studies (Kratochwill & Shernoff, 2003) or research across classrooms, students, and settings to assess the external validity (Campbell & Stanley, 1966) and/or transportability (Shoenwald & Hoagwood, 2001) of the TTG.

One limitation of interdependent group reinforcement programs is that individual students could sabotage the group (Skinner, Cashwell, & Dunn, 1996). The current intervention was extremely susceptible to sabotage as one student could remain standing and the entire group would suffer. This, in fact, occurred. Specifically, on one day, a student who had gotten into trouble in the lunchroom decided to sabotage the game by not sitting down. The student stood for nearly 2 minutes, causing the class to miss their randomly selected transition criterion and ultimately, not get a letter. The entire class knew that the timer would not be turned off until everyone was seated and verbally prompted (requested, reasoned with, begged, and/or demanded) the student to sit. While peers did not threaten the saboteur, this could have occurred when he did not respond to their prompts.

To reduce the likelihood of sabotage, Skinner et al. (1996) recommend forming a pool of reinforcers, so that for each student, one or more high quality reinforcers are in the pool. Reinforcers are then randomly selected. While such procedures could reduce instances of sabotage because no student would want to risk not earning a high quality reinforcer, experimental research is needed to determine if such procedures do indeed reduce instances of sabotage. Regardless, in the current study, the teacher merely ignored the saboteur's behavior, monitored peers for inappropriate behavior (e.g., threats, name-calling), and let peers attempt to alter this student's behavior. These procedures appeared to work as this student did not sabotage the group the remainder of the school year.

By using experimental procedures the current study showed that the TTG decreased lunch-to-classroom transitions times with the participants in this study. The TTG is comprised of multiple components including (a) explicit timing, (b) public posting, and (c) an interdependent group-oriented contingency. Each of these components has been shown to cause changes in student behavior. Therefore, component analysis studies are needed to determine the degree of influence each component had on student transition times. As such studies more precisely assess the impact of each component on student transition behaviors, they have clear theoretical implications. Additionally, if component analysis studies show that some components are ineffective, practitioners may be able to more efficiently implement the TTG. For example, if the group reinforcement was not needed, then the program could be implemented with fewer resources. Therefore, future researchers should consider conducting component analysis studies of the TTG.

CONCLUSION

When discussing a science of human behavior we often use the term research, as opposed to search. In the current study, we re-searched the Campbell and Skinner empirical case study. However, this does not mean that the Campbell and Skinner study should be thought of as an initial search, as the TTG was not totally novel. Instead, Campbell and Skinner developed the TTG by applying previous basic research (e.g., laboratory research on reinforcement) and applied research (there have been many studies of interdependent group reinforcement and explicit timing in educational settings) to address a presenting problem. Thus, the efficacy of each component of the TTG had been established by previous researchers using scientific procedures. This is not uncommon as many effective interventions are based on theories, strategies, and procedures that have been empirically validated, empirically supported, and/or are evidence-based (Kratochwill & Shernoff, 2003; Kratochwill & Stoiber, 2000a,b). Thus, the initial Campbell and Skinner empirical case study was not search, but *re*search as the practitioners relied on and applied previous science to develop and guide intervention development.

Campbell and Skinner were asked to address a problem in a classroom. They used previous applied and theoretical research to develop a multiple component intervention, the TTG. Additionally, they collected baseline and intervention phase data. These data had applied value because they allowed the practitioners to determine whether the target behavior was improving. Unfortunately, from a scientific perspective, these data did not allow for the establishment of cause-and-effect relationships. However, Campbell and Skinner's initial empirical case study did have scientific value (i.e., heuristic value) because it provided evidence that the TTG may have been effective and encouraged us to conduct the current scientific study designed to assess the effects of the intervention.

REFERENCES

Campbell, S., & Skinner, C. H. (2004). Combining explicit timing with an interdependent group contingency program to decrease transition times: An investigation of the timely transitions game. *Journal of Applied School Psychology, 20*(2), 11-27.

Campbell, D. T., & Stanley, J. C. (1966). *Experimental and quasi-experimental designs for research.* Chicago: Rand McNally.

Derr, T. F., & Shapiro, E. S. (1989). A behavioral evaluation of curriculum-based assessment of reading. *Journal of Psychoeducational Assessment, 7*, 148-160.

Derr-Minneci, T. F., & Shapiro, E. S. (1992). Validating curriculum-based measurement in reading from a behavioral perspective. *School Psychology Quarterly, 7*, 2-16.

Elliott, S. N. (1988). Acceptability of behavioral treatments in educational settings. In J. C. Witt, S. N. Elliott, & F. M. Gresham (Eds.), *Handbook of behavior therapy in education* (pp. 121-150). New York: Plenum.

Evans, T., Skinner, C. H., & Henington, C., Sims, S., & McDaniel, E. C. (2002). Conspicuous and covert timing during CBM of mathematics across African-American and Caucasian students: An investigation of situational bias. *School Psychology Review, 31*, 529-539.

Freeland, J. T., & Noell, G. H. (1999). Maintaining accurate math response in elementary students: The effects of delayed and intermittent reinforcement and programming common stimuli. *Journal of Applied Behavior Analysis, 32*, 211-215.

Freeland, J. T., & Noell, G. H. (2002). Programming for maintenance: An investigation of delayed and intermittent reinforcement and common stimuli to create indiscriminable contingencies. *Journal of Behavioral Education, 11*, 5-18.

Greenwood, C. R., Delquadri, J. C., & Carta, J. J. (1997). Together we can! Classwide peer tutoring to improve basic academic skills. Longmont, CO: Sopris West.

Gresham, F. M. (1989). Assessment of treatment integrity in school consultation and prereferral intervention. *School Psychology Quarterly, 18*, 37-50.

Gresham, F. M., & Gresham, G. N. (1982). Interdependent, dependent, and independent group contingencies for controlling disruptive behavior. *Journal of Special Education, 16*, 101-110.

Hersen, M., & Barlow, D. H. (1982). *Single case experimental designs: Strategies for studying behavior change.* New York: Pergamon Press.

Johnson, S. M., & Bolstad, O. D. (1973). Methodological issues in naturalistic observation: Some problems and solutions. In L. A. Hamerlynck, L. E. Handy, & E. J. Mash (Eds.), *Behavior change: Methodology, concepts, and practices* (pp. 7-68). Champaign, IL: Research Press.

Kelshaw-Levering, K., Sterling-Turner, H. E., Henry, J. R., & Skinner, C. H. (2000). Randomized interdependent group contingencies: Group reinforcement with a twist. *Psychology in the Schools, 37*, 523-533.

Kratochwill, T. R., & Shernoff, E. S. (2003). Evidence-based practice: Promoting evidence-based interventions in school psychology. *School Psychology Quarterly, 18,* 389-408.

Kratochwill, T. R., & Stoiber, K. C. (2000a). Diversifying theory and science: Expanding boundaries of empirically supported interventions in schools. *Journal of School Psychology, 38,* 349-358.

Kratochwill, T. R., & Stoiber, K. C. (2000b). Empirically supported interventions and school psychology: Conceptual and practical issues: Part II. *School Psychology Quarterly, 15,* 233-253.

Lew, M., Mesch, D., Johnson, D. W., & Johnson, R. (1986). Positive interdependence, academic and collaborative-skills group contingencies and isolated students. *American Educational Research Journal, 23,* 341-347.

McGill, R. (1999). Establishing operations: Implications for the assessment, treatment, and prevention of problem behavior. *Journal of Applied Behavior Analysis, 25,* 393-418.

Michael, J. (1993). Establishing operations. *The Behavior Analyst, 16,* 191-206.

Moore, L. A., Waguespack, A. M., Wickstrom, K. F., Witt, J. C., & Gaydos, G. R. (1994). Mystery motivator: An effective and time efficient intervention. *School Psychology Review, 23,* 106-118.

Noell, G. H., & Witt, J. C. (1998). Toward a behavior analytic approach to consultation. In T. S. Watson & F. M. Gresham (Eds.), *Handbook of child behavior therapy* (pp. 41-57). New York: Plenum Press.

Popkin, J., & Skinner, C. H. (2003). Enhancing academic performance in a classroom serving students with serious emotional disturbance: Interdependent group contingencies with randomly selected components. *School Psychology Review, 32,* 282-295.

Rhymer, K. N., Henington, C., Skinner, C. H., & Looby, E. J. (1999). The effects of explicit timing on mathematics performance in Caucasian and African-American second-grade students. *School Psychology Quarterly, 14,* 397-407.

Rhymer, K. N., Skinner, C. H., Henington, C., D'Reaux, R. A., & Sims, S. (1998). Effects of explicit timing on mathematics problem completion rates in African-American third-grade elementary students. *Journal of Applied Behavior Analysis, 31,* 673-677.

Rhymer, K. N., Skinner, C. H., Jackson, S., McNeill, S., Smith, T., & Jackson, B. (2002). The 1-minute explicit timing intervention: The influence of mathematics problem difficulty. *Journal of Instructional Psychology, 29,* 305-312.

Romeo, F. F. (1998). The negative effects of using a group contingency system of classroom management. *Journal of Instructional Psychology, 25,* 130-133.

Shoenwald, S. K., & Hoagwood, K. (2001). Effectiveness, transportability and dissemination of interventions: What matters when? *Psychiatric Services, 52,* 1190-1197.

Skinner, C. H., Cashwell, C. S., & Dunn, M. S. (1996). Independent and interdependent group contingencies: Smoothing the rough waters. *Special Services in the Schools, 12,* 198-215.

Skinner, C. H., Skinner, A. L., & Sterling-Turner, H. E. (2002). Best practices in utilizing group contingencies for intervention and prevention. In A. Thomas & J. Grimes

(Eds.), *Best Practices in school psychology (4th ed)* (817-830). Washington, D.C.: National Association of School Psychologists.

Skinner, C. H., Waterson, H. J., Bryant, D. R., Bryant, R. J., Collins, P. M., Hill, C. J., Tipton, M. F., Ragsdale, P., & Fox, J. (2002). Team problem solving based on research, functional behavioral assessment data, teacher acceptability, and Jim Carey's Interview. *Proven Practices: Prevention & Remediation Solutions for Schools, 4,* 56-64.

Skinner, C. H., Williams, R. L., & Neddenriep, C. E. (in press). The negative side effects of rewarding academic behavior: Problems revisited and resolved via randomizing interdependent group contingency components. *School Psychology Review.*

Slavin, R. E. (1987). Cooperative learning: Where behavioral and humanistic approaches to classroom management meet. *The Elementary School Journal, 88,* 29-37.

Smith, R. G., & Iwata, B. (1997). Antecedent influences on behavior disorders. *Journal of Applied Behavior Analysis, 30,* 343-375.

Stage, S. A., & Quiroz, D. R. (1997). A meta-analysis of interventions to decrease disruptive classroom behavior in public education settings. *School Psychology Review, 26,* 333-368.

Theodore, L. A., Bray, M., Kehle, T. J., & Jenson, W. (2001). Randomization of Group Contingencies and Reinforcers to Reduce Classroom Disruptive Behavior. *Journal of School Psychology, 39,* 267-277.

Turco, T. L., & Elliott, S. N. (1986). Assessment of students' acceptability of teacher-initiated interventions for classroom misbehavior. *Journal of School Psychology, 24,* 307-313.

Turco, T. L., & Elliott, S. N. (1990). Acceptability and effectiveness of group contingencies for improving spelling achievement. *Journal of School Psychology, 28,* 27-37.

Van Houten, R., Hill, S., & Parsons, M. (1975). An analysis of a performance feedback system: The effects of timing and feedback, public posting, and praise upon academic performance and peer interaction. *Journal of Applied Behavior Analysis, 12,* 581-591.

Van Houten, R., & Thompson, C. (1976). The effects of explicit timing on math performance. *Journal of Applied Behavior Analysis, 9,* 227-230.

Von Brock, M. B., & Elliott, S. N. (1987). The influence of treatment effectiveness information on the acceptability of classroom interventions. *Journal of School Psychology, 25,* 131-144.

Witt, J. C., & Elliott, S. N. (1985). Acceptability of classroom management strategies. In T. R. Kratochwill (Ed.), *Advances in school psychology* (Vol. 4, pp. 251-288). Hillsdale, NJ: Erlbaum.

Witt, J. C., Gresham, F. M., & Noell, G. H. (1996). What's behavioral about behavioral consultation? *Journal of Educational and Psychological Consultation, 7,* 327-344.

Zins, J., & Ponti, C. (1990). Best practice in school-based consultation. In A. Thomas & J. Grimes (Eds.), *Best practices in school psychology* (2nd Ed., pp. 673-693). Washington, DC: National Association of School Psychologists.

Practicing School Consultants Can Empirically Validate Interventions: A Description and Demonstration of the Non-Concurrent Multiple-Baseline Design

Beth D. Winn
Christopher H. Skinner
Jessica D. Allin
James A. Hawkins

University of Tennessee

SUMMARY. The purpose of this manuscript is to describe and demonstrate how practicing school psychologists who are serving as consultants can empirically validate interventions using the non-concurrent multiple-baseline across-subjects (Non-Con M-B A-S) design. Over the course of a school year, three teachers, from different elementary schools, each referred a student for behavioral consultation. In each case, the target problem was insufficient journal writing, and the teacher and consultant developed interventions consisting of goal setting, self-monitoring, self-graphing, and

---

Address correspondence to: Christopher H. Skinner, PhD, The University of Tennessee, College of EHHS, Claxton Complex A-518, Knoxville, TN 37996-3452 (E-mail: cskinne1@utk.edu).

[Haworth co-indexing entry note]: "Practicing School Consultants Can Empirically Validate Interventions: A Description and Demonstration of the Non-Concurrent Multiple-Baseline Design." Winn et al. Co-published simultaneously in *Journal of Applied School Psychology* (The Haworth Press, Inc.) Vol. 20, No. 2, 2004, pp. 109-128; and: *Single-Subject Designs for School Psychologists* (ed: Christopher H. Skinner) The Haworth Press, Inc., 2004, pp. 109-128. Single or multiple copies of this article are available for a fee from The Haworth Document Delivery Service [1-800-HAWORTH, 9:00 a.m. - 5:00 p.m. (EST). E-mail address: docdelivery@haworthpress.com].

Digital Object Identifier: 10.1300/J008v20n02_07

109

reinforcement. Data from the three behavioral consultation cases were combined to form a Non-Con M-B A-S design. Results showed immediate and sustained increases in students' journal writing after the intervention was implemented. Discussion focuses on applied and experimental strengths and limitations associated with practicing school consultants' use of the Non-Con M-B A-S design. *[Article copies available for a fee from The Haworth Document Delivery Service: 1-800-HAWORTH. E-mail address: <docdelivery@haworthpress.com> Website: <http://www.HaworthPress.com> © 2004 by The Haworth Press, Inc. All rights reserved.]*

KEYWORDS. Writing, self-management, non-concurrent multiple-baseline design, behavioral consultation, practitioner research

School psychologists are committed to remedying student problems with procedures that are supported with theoretical and applied science (Hughes, 2000; Shapiro, 1996; Stoiber & Kratochwill, 2000). In addition to consuming research related to empirically supported interventions, some specific models of service delivery may allow school psychologists to contribute to this science with data collected during their professional practice. Behavioral consultation (BC) is a model for delivering science-supported interventions that requires the collection of within-subject, repeated measures data (Bergan, 1977; Bergan & Kratochwill, 1990). These data have applied value in that they can be used to evaluate intervention effects. However, because these data are often limited to baseline and intervention phase data (i.e., an empirical A-B design), there is little control for threats to internal validity (Barlow & Hersen, 1984). Thus, while the intervention may account for measured changes in behavior, it is also possible that other variables (i.e., uncontrolled threats to internal validity) account for recorded changes in student behavior. These uncontrolled threats to internal validity prevent one from establishing cause-and-effect relationships between interventions and behavior change. This limits the opportunities for practicing behavioral consultants to contribute to the scientific process of validating interventions (Hayes, 1985).

Several single-subject research designs address this problem, but have limitations that make it difficult for school consultants to apply these designs in educational settings. For example, withdrawal designs (i.e., A-B-A-B phases) can control for threats to internal validity. However, demonstration of experimental control (i.e., demonstrating that the intervention caused the change) requires target behaviors return toward baseline levels during the second A-phase. This requirement is often unacceptable to educators, parents, and students who may refuse to implement procedures that cause a student's behaviors to revert towards pre-treatment levels (see Campbell and Skinner, this volume, for an example of this limitation). Additionally, in school settings many target behaviors may not reverse. For example, once a student is taught academic skills, they often will continue to successfully complete those academic tasks even after interventions are withdrawn (Sindelar, Rosenberg, & Wilson, 1985).

An alternative to withdrawal designs is the concurrent multiple-baseline across-subjects (Con M-B A-S) design. This design does not require practitioner-researchers (e.g., teacher and consultant) to first improve a student's behavior and then implement procedures that make it worse (e.g., abruptly withdraw the intervention). Because behaviors are not required to reverse, this design is useful when targeting behaviors that are unlikely to reverse when the treatment is withdrawn. The Con M-B A-S design is similar to a series of three or more A-B phase empirical case studies, where similar dependent variables and intervention procedures are used across subjects (three or more). With the Con M-B A-S design, data is collected across all subjects' behaviors concurrently and typically in the same setting with the same treatment agents (Baer, Wolf, & Risley, 1968) with baseline phase lengths varied across subjects (i.e., application of treatments across subjects is staggered over time).

The Con M-B A-S design is superior to a series of across subject A-B replications (Rickards-Schlichting, Kehle, and Bray, this volume, provides an example) because experimental procedures can control for threats to internal validity (Kazdin & Kopel, 1975). The possibility that some uncontrolled extraneous event occurred that caused desired change in behavior at approximately the same time the intervention was implemented (i.e., history effect) are assessed by making comparisons across subjects (Campbell & Stanley, 1963). When the intervention is first implemented with one student, the experimenter continues to collect baseline data (concurrent data) on the other students who have not yet been exposed to the treatment. If the treated student's behavior improves, it could have been caused by the treatment. However, improvements may have been caused by other events that may have occurred in the classroom or in the student's community at approximately the same time the intervention was implemented. If some extraneous variable(s) caused these changes, similar changes may occur in the behavior of students who are still in the baseline or no-treatment phase. If this occurs, history effects cannot be ruled out, as there is empirical evidence that something other than the treatment may have caused the change in the treated student's behavior.

In addition to *assessing* for history effects, staggering the implementation of treatments across time helps rule out history effects via the principle of successive coincidences (Barlow & Hersen, 1984; Hayes, 1985). Across three or more students, it is unreasonable to assume that an uncontrolled extraneous variable would cause changes in each student's behavior at different times, and those times coincide with the application of treatments to each student. Thus, staggering the implementation of the treatments across subsequent students (i.e., those in baseline) allows for repeated demonstration of experimental control and repeated assessment of history effects (Harris & Jenson, 1985).

Staggering interventions also allows one to assess for testing effects, instrumentation, and other threats to internal validity associated with assessment procedures (e.g., reactivity, observer drift, practice effects, fatigue). If assessment procedures caused changes in one student's behavior (e.g., testing effects), similar changes should occur in the behaviors of the students who have not yet received the treatment (i.e., those students still in baseline). Likewise, if the assessment procedures changed as the result of repeated assessments (e.g., observer drift), similar changes should occur in the data of students who have not yet received the treatment (Hayes, 1985).

The Con M-B A-S design can be used when consultants receive three concurrent referrals, for similar target behaviors, across three different students, and the treatment and procedures for measuring the effects of the treatment are similar. Assessment of history effects is strongest when these students are likely to be exposed to similar extraneous variables that may impact target behaviors (i.e., student from the same classroom and community who have the same teacher).

While school psychologists serving as consultants may occasionally receive simultaneous referrals, from the same teacher, for the same problem, and across three or more classmates, there are several reasons why this design may not be appropriate or acceptable. When using the Con M-B A-S design, demonstration of experimental control requires that the treatment affect the target behavior of the treated student, but not the behavior of his classmates who are in the baseline phase. When a student is being treated in a classroom, there is the possibility of spillover effects, where the treatment affects a classmate who has not yet received the treatment. For example, John may receive strategy training (treatment) in solving math problems. While Ralph is still in baseline, John may teach Ralph the strategy. Co-variation also may occur when treated and untreated students are in the same classroom. For example, suppose Manny, Moe, and Jack often fight. A treatment introduced to decrease Manny's fighting is likely to cause concurrent reductions in fighting in Moe and Jack, because Manny is no longer initiating fighting.

Even when co-variation and spillover effects are improbable, often there are other applied problems associated with school-based consultants implementing Con M-B A-S designs in educational settings. Often when a teacher refers multiple students for the same behavior problems, practical (e.g., saving time and resources) and ethical (e.g., withholding treatment from two or more students until the first student targeted shows improvement) concerns may prevent consultants from staggering intervention implementation across students (Hayes, 1985). Additionally, the requirement to use treatments that only affect one student's behavior at a time places a severe and perhaps unethical limitation on intervention selection. For example, many class-wide treatments (e.g., group contingencies, collaborative learning, curricula changes) could prove to be the most effective and efficient way to prevent problems across students. However, because they would alter all students' behaviors simultaneously, the interventions could not be evaluated using a Con M-B A-S.

The Non-Concurrent Multiple-Baseline Design

School psychologists, serving as consultants, are likely to receive referrals for similar problems across students. However, these referrals often come at different times and from different teachers. In these instances, school psychologists using BC may be able to use non-concurrent multiple-baseline across-subjects (Non-Con M-B A-S) designs to control for many threats to internal validity while addressing practical limitations associated with other designs (Watson & Workman, 1981). This design is similar to the Con M-B A-S design, in that baseline phase lengths are staggered across subjects. However, as the name of the design implies, demonstrations of experimental control do not require that the cases be conducted concurrently. Thus, the Non-Con M-B A-S design may allow school psychologists to contribute to the evaluation of interventions by combining consultation data across cases (e.g., different students, teachers, and classrooms) and over time.

As with the Con M-B A-S design, the Non-Con M-B A-S design controls for testing effects, instrumentation, and other threats to internal validity associated with assessment procedures (e.g., practice effects, observer drift) by staggering baseline lengths across students (Watson & Workman, 1981). However, unlike the Con M-B A-S, the non-concurrent design does not *assess* for history effects. Although this limitation is a concern, in many situations history effects are less likely to impact Non-Con M-B A-S designs than Con M-B A-S designs. For example, a school psychologist and teacher may develop and implement an effective, acceptable, and efficient intervention to address a specific problem. Over time, the same school psychologist may get similar referrals to address the same problem (a) in different students, (b) from different teachers, and (c) in different classrooms, schools, and communities. In this situation, it is reasonable to assume that school psychologists may influence the consultation process so that the effective, acceptable, and efficient intervention is used in these subsequent cases. Furthermore, it is unreasonable to assume that an extraneous event(s) would occur and cause a change in target behaviors at approximately the same time the intervention was implemented in each of these *different settings*, across *different teachers*, and at *different times* (Hayes, 1985; Watson & Workman, 1981). Thus, although the Non-Con M-B A-S design does not assess for history effects, it is also less susceptible to history effects. Additionally, when the three students are from three different classrooms and/or schools, being treated by three different educators, at three different times, spillover effects and covariation also are highly improbable.

There are two other limitations associated with practicing consultants applying the Non-Con M-B A-S design. First, there is the possibility that from the pool of previous cases, only cases that work may be selected and included in the study.[1] This limitation is significant. However, the failure to disseminate findings that do not show a change in behavior is not limited to this design but is a serious threat to the entire process of attempting to empirically validate interventions. Second, there is a possibility that consultants would wait to implement interventions until something else occurs in the environment or within the child that is likely to cause or support the desired behavior change. If this is the case, changes in behavior may be caused by these extraneous variable(s), the intervention, or an interaction of these variables. One suggestion for control for this problem is to randomly assign baseline phase lengths to participants (Watson & Workman, 1981). While this suggestion may be reasonable, applied considerations often influence baseline length. For example, teachers, school psychologists, parents, and school administrators may find implementing a randomly selected extended baseline phase unacceptable, because such procedures require withholding treatments. This may be particularly true for problems that are more serious or when data is trending in an undesired direction (i.e., the problem is getting more severe). Additionally, decisions regarding when to begin implementing treatments are often based on practical matters such as (a) when the school psychologist and teacher can meet to design interventions, (b) the amount of training needed to carry out the interventions, and (c) when materials can be constructed or obtained that are needed for the interventions.

The Current Study

Despite recent repeated calls for the use of empirically validated or supported interventions, Robinson, Skinner, and Brown (1998) found school psychology journals contained few experimental studies that attempt to empirically validate interventions. The primary purpose of the current study is to demonstrate how the Non-Con M-B A-S design may allow practicing school psychologists to contribute to the process of developing and validating interventions by combining BC data across cases in a manner that controls for threats to internal validity.

The current study combines data from three BC cases designed to enhance journal writing productivity. Journal writing is one strategy that is often used to develop expressive writing skills, including handwriting fluency, vocabulary, sentence structure, and other writing skills (Borasi & Rose, 1989; Hoover, 1979). While allocating time for journal writing activities may enhance written expression skills in some students (Christenson, Thurlow, Ysseldyke, & McVicar, 1989), as with any other academic intervention procedure, some students will not benefit from these practice opportunities because they will choose not to write (Skinner, 2002).

Student-derived and teacher-derived goals can improve students' academic productivity (Kelley & Stokes, 1984; Lee & Tindal, 1994). Goal setting interventions have been shown to be more effective when teachers provide feedback, praise, and additional high quality reinforcers for increased productivity (Caldwell, Wolery, Werts, & Caldwell, 1996; Kazdin, 1974; McLaughlin, 1992; Neef, Shade, & Miller, 1994). Soliciting each student's input regarding reinforcers that he or she would like to earn may allow for the identification of idiosyncratic high quality reinforcers and allow students to feel they have control over proceedings in the classroom (Young, West, Li, & Peterson, 1997). The effectiveness of these strategies can be enhanced with self-monitoring procedures, including students observing, recording, evaluating, and graphing their own behaviors (Daniels & Hansen, 1976; DiGangi, Maag, & Rutherford, 1991; Maag, Rutherford, & DiGangi, 1992; Moxley, Lutz, Ahlborn, Boley, & Armstrong, 1995; Seabaugh & Schumaker, 1994; Shimabukro, Prater, Jenkins, & Edelen-Smith, 1999; Trammel, Schloss, & Alper, 1994). In the current study, goal setting, self-monitoring, praise, feedback and other student-selected reinforcers were combined in an attempt to enhance journal writing.

METHOD

Participants and Setting

Participants in this study included three elementary school students. Each student was enrolled in a different general education classroom in a different inner city school. Each school served a low-income area of a southeastern city. Over 70% of the students at each school received reduced or free lunch. Each general education classroom contained 15-19 students. A different consultant worked with each teacher. The teachers had between 3 and 25 years of teaching experience. Consultants were school psychology graduate students.

Brian was a 9-year-old African-American male enrolled in the fourth grade. Diana was a 7-year-old African-American female enrolled in the first grade. Chris was a 7-year-old Caucasian male enrolled in the first grade. Three separate teachers, from three different schools, referred these students for behavioral consultation during the same academic school year. In each case, the referral problem was insufficient journal writing. Although Chris's teacher reported his academic achievement as average compared to his peers, Brian and Diana were reported to be academically behind the majority of their classmates.

General Procedures

While it is beyond the scope of the current paper to describe all the BC procedures followed for each case, Bergan and Kratochwill's (1990) model provided the basic steps of the process. For each case, a teacher referred a student for poor performance during journal writing and each teacher-consultant dyad developed, implemented, and evaluated a procedure designed to enhance journal writing. While the dyads worked independently, the consultees met weekly with a professor for group supervision where BC cases were reviewed. Thus, the three consultants shared information regarding interventions. However, for each case the classroom teacher and consultant developed their interventions and the teacher had final and ultimate authority for making all decisions (e.g., data collection and intervention procedures).

Research Design

The current study is composed of three A-B designs. No specific plans were made to carry out an experimental study. However, because the three interventions used similar intervention strategies and the same dependent variable, each case involved a replication. Because the interventions were implemented at different times and baseline lengths varied, again unintentionally, the three cases were combined to form a non-concurrent multiple-baseline across subjects design (Watson & Workman, 1981). This design can provide greater evidence of generalization (external validity) and is less likely to be impacted by history effects (threat to internal validity) than the concurrent multiple-baseline design (Barlow & Hersen, 1984).

Materials

In each of the three cases, a chart was used to provide visual progress and performance feedback. For Brian and Diana, a chart drawn in the shape of a thermometer was used to record the words written each day. These two charts were laminated and markers were used to color the corresponding number written on each chart. Chris's chart was created in the shape of a football field using green poster board. A plastic football was used to identify the number of words he wrote each day. Each student kept completed journal assignments in either a folder or binder. Consultants also kept a recording sheet for the number of words written each day for their target students.

Pre-Intervention Procedures (Baseline)

Each class engaged in a daily journal writing assignment. In each class, students were seated in their assigned seats. The teacher would instruct students to take out their journals and then the teacher would write a story starter such as, "My favorite thing about spring is . . . " on the black or white board. Students then wrote the story starter and continued to write in the journal. For Brian's class, journal writing was the first activity each day and students were given 30 minutes for journal writing. Chris's class also began the day with journal writing and wrote for ten minutes. Diana's class also had 30 minutes allotted for journal writing from 11:20-11:50.

Dependent Variable

The dependent variable for each case was the number of words written. At various times during the cases, students (self-monitoring), teachers (checking student work), consultants, and independent observers (interscorer agreement) counted words written. For the current study, the dependent variable was based on consultant counts. Consultants collected journal folders two to five times per week and counted the number of words written each day. Additionally, they photocopied the pages (a new page was used each day) in order to collect interscorer agreement data. To be included as a word, the consultant merely had to recognize it as a word. The word did not have to be spelled correctly or used appropriately (e.g., grammar was not considered). Additionally, if two of the same words were used consecutively, they were not counted (e.g., It rained very very very very very very hard).

Intervention

A goal chart was constructed for each student. On Brian's goal chart, the goal (30 words written) was written at the top of the thermometer. A scale with increments of five words was written along the side of the thermometer (e.g., 5, 10, 15, 20, 25). Diana's goal chart was similarly marked but since her goals changed during the intervention, the goal also changed on her chart as well as the increments. Diana's goals were based on words written over cumulative days. Because Chris enjoyed football, a football field was used as his goal chart. A plastic football was placed on the twenty-yard line on the football field each day and his goal was to score a touchdown by moving one yard towards the end zone for each word written.

Prior to beginning the intervention, each student's teacher and consultant reviewed each student's baseline data and peers' data and set goals. For Brian and Chris, goals were based on daily performance. Brian's goal was 30 words each day. Chris's goal was 20 words each day. For Diana, a cumulative goal was used where she would receive access to reinforcement when her total number of words across 5 days reached this goal. The first goal was 50 words, the second was 100, and the third was 150.

For each student, the teacher and consultant met to select reinforcers that could easily be delivered with little disruption to classroom routines and were judged to be high quality reinforcers for each target student. Brian received 15 minutes of computer time, typically at the end of each day, when he met his daily goal. Chris received either computer time (when time was available at the end of the day) or crayons each day he met his goal. Diana received a soft drink during lunch when she met her first goal and a pencil, eraser, or notebook for meeting her second and third goals.

After materials were prepared and goals and reinforcers established, the teacher met with each student to review procedures. Specifically, when journal writing time ended each student was taught to count and record the number of words written during the daily journal assignment. Next, they were taught to record this data on their goal charts. Brian and Diana colored to the corresponding number of words each day. Chris moved his football one yard for each word. Students were instructed to raise their hand and inform the teacher when they met their goal. Because Diana's goal was cumulative and designed to be met over several days, she was instructed to raise her hand and inform the teacher when she had a "good journal writing day." In addition to delivering idiosyncratic reinforcers for goal attainment, teachers were instructed to check each student's word counts for accuracy and praise students for productive writing.

Interscorer Agreement

Consultant word counts served as the primary dependent variable. Using photocopies, an independent observer scored 54% of the daily journal assignments. Percent interscorer agreement was calculated for each assignment on a word-by-word basis by dividing the number of agreements by the number of agreements plus disagreements and multiplying by 100. Percent interscorer agreement ranged from 82%-100% ($\chi = 92\%$). In almost all instances disagreements were caused by difficulty scoring sloppy writing.

RESULTS

Figure 1 displays the number of words written each school day across all three students during baseline and intervention phases. Brian wrote no words during journal activities during the baseline phase. Immediately after the intervention was implemented, Brian increased his journal productivity to over 30 words until the third intervention day when Brian wrote no words. The teacher reported that Brian was involved in an incident earlier in the school day and refused to do any work after that incident. After this day, there was a steady increase in the number of words written. Average words written per day increased from 0 during baseline to 26 during the intervention. Brian met his daily goal of at least 30 words 5 of 7 intervention days.

During baseline, Chris wrote an average of five words per day in his journal. There was no trend in Chris's word productivity during baseline. Figure 1 shows an immediate increase in Chris's productivity following the implementation of the intervention. During the intervention Chris averaged 25 words per day (range 17 to 47). Chris's performance was less stable during the intervention phase. However, each intervention day Chris's productivity exceeded his best performance during baseline by at least 100%. Chris met his goal on 8 of 10 intervention days.

During baseline, Diana averaged seven words written in her daily journal. During the intervention, Diana increased this average to 29 words a day. Figure 1 shows a slightly increasing trend in journal writing during baseline. Immediately after the intervention was implemented, Diana's writing increased over 100% from her best baseline performance. During the intervention phase, a brief increasing trend immediately after the intervention was implemented was followed by a decreasing trend in productivity. At this point the consultant met with the teacher to evaluate the intervention. The teacher reported that she had not given Diana her reinforcer when she met her second cumulative goal and did not consistently review and praise Diana's productivity. After this meeting, the consultant met with the student and reminded her to raise her hand and show her teacher her progress using the thermometer goal chart. An increasing trend developed after reinforcement was provided more consistently. Diana's daily number of words ranged from 14 to 67 words during the intervention.

DISCUSSION

Applied Implications

Three different elementary school teachers who allotted time each school day for journal writing activities referred students for insuffi-

FIGURE 1. Words Written During Baseline and Intervention Phase Across Students

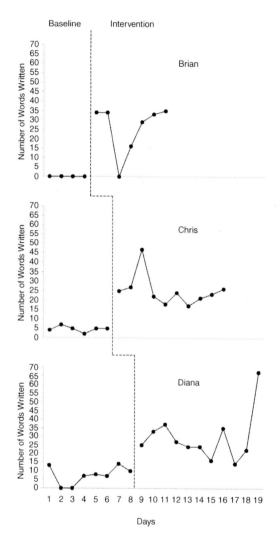

cient journal writing. The current study suggests that the intervention increased journal writing productivity across students, classrooms, schools, teachers, consultants, and grade levels. Although this study did not measure or target writing quality, results suggest that this intervention increased writing quantity. Now that the students are choosing to write, the next step would be to develop procedures to address writing quality. Future researchers should conduct longitudinal studies to determine if such procedures enhance students' skill development enough to result in educationally valid increases in writing skills.

During evaluation interviews, all three teachers commented on the improvements of their students. Each reported that the intervention was easy to implement and required few resources and little teacher time. All three teachers reported that their students liked the intervention. Each teacher indicated that the students appeared to enjoy counting and recording words written and often solicited teacher praise after they recorded their word counts. Brian's teacher indicated that she observed Brian sharing his success with his peers. Unlike his classmates, prior to the intervention Brian had no completed journal assignments in his folder. As he began adding assignments to his folder, Brian began soliciting praise by showing the folder to his classmates. Diana's teacher reported that Diana seemed to be improving her performance in other academic areas. These reports suggest that future researchers should conduct systematic studies designed to evaluate teacher and student acceptability of the current interventions and possible positive side effects associated with the interventions.

In the current study, each specific strategy may have played a vital role in the improvements seen in these students. Goals were set to be attainable but challenging for each student. Working towards established goals seemed to motivate each student. Students appeared to respond well to positive teacher feedback as they often solicited this feedback after they recorded word counts. Prior to the intervention, each student had experienced low levels of success with journal writing activities. During the intervention, both the teacher and student appeared to enjoy focusing on positive aspects of the student's writing. The self-evaluating and self-recording of words written daily may have contributed to the success of the intervention by encouraging the students to take ownership over their progress and performance, while also making the intervention more manageable for each teacher. Prior to the intervention, each student expressed a dislike for journal writing. Thus, the additional idiosyncratic tangible or activity rewards for meeting goals may have been needed to increase the strength of this intervention.

Design Issues and Limitations

There are several limitations associated with the current study that should be addressed by future researchers. First, because all intervention components (e.g., goal settings, self-monitoring, self-graphing, and reinforcement) have been shown to be effective in increasing productivity, it is not possible to determine which specific intervention component or which combination of components caused the increases in journal writing productivity. This limitation is significant and is likely to occur within applied settings where the primary goal is for the consultant and teacher to develop effective treatments. Regardless, this limitation occurs often in applied educational settings where it is difficult to conduct a pure study of the effects of a single treatment. For example, when any behavior is targeted that is likely to be supported or reinforced in the student's natural environment, the change in that behavior may be partially attributed to the intervention and partially attributed to this environmental support that is accessed as the behavior changes (McConnell, 1987; Stokes & Baer, 1977). Thus, while implementing a single-procedure intervention may limit interaction effects, these interactions are still likely to occur in applied settings. Regardless, future component analysis studies that specify component effects may have theoretical implications and also assist practitioners by allowing them to construct more resource efficient interventions.

A second limitation is that consultants were not available to conduct direct observations with respect to treatment integrity. Again, this is a common problem associated with consultation. In the current study, problems with integrity became apparent when Diana's teacher reported that she had not provided the reinforcer once Diana met her second goal. Although the failure to collect treatment integrity data is a limitation, the severity of this limitation is dependent upon outcomes. When treatments are found to be ineffective, taking data on specific treatment behaviors will allow one to determine if poor treatment integrity *may* account for ineffective treatments. Thus, treatment integrity data is necessary to help prevent Type II error, which is to erroneously conclude that the treatment was ineffective.

In the current study, the students' behavior did improve. Thus, concerns focus on Type I error, concluding the treatment was effective when something else caused the change. Since we do not know all the events that may affect any target behavior,[2] there is no way to collect data (e.g., treatment integrity data) on all the other extraneous events that may have caused the change. Instead, experimental procedures are used to rule out these effects. Earlier, we described how the Non-Con M-B A-S design controls for threats to internal validity. The large change in target behaviors (number of words written) *immediately* after the intervention was implemented across all three students attending three different classrooms and schools, with three different teachers and three different consultants, makes it unreasonable to assume that some extraneous variable caused these changes (Hayes, 1985).

In the current study, the three cases used similar strategies; however, the interventions were not identical across cases. Different goals, reinforcers, and self-monitoring procedures were established for each student based on baseline performance, teacher perceptions and judgments, and the consultation process. Again, this limitation is infrequently controlled in applied educational research (Hayes, 1985). For example, in an attempt to keep intervention procedures identical, researchers could have held reinforcement constant across students. However, a specific stimulus (e.g., telling a student "good job" after meeting a goal) may be a high quality or strong reinforcer for one student and a weak reinforcer, a neutral stimulus, or even an aversive stimulus for another student. Thus, although holding consequent stimuli constant across students has the appearance of using identical interventions, often researchers are actually implementing qualitatively different interventions when they use identical procedures.

Another limitation is that baseline phase lengths were not randomly assigned across cases. This procedure is recommended by Watson and Workman (1981) to control for experimenters (consultants and teachers in this case) implementing interventions at a time when data or conditions suggest that something else within the environment or child is about to occur which will cause the behavior to improve. While this concern may be valid in some instances, because the current cases were not designed as an experiment, baseline lengths were not intentionally varied across cases. Rather, baseline phase lengths were selected based on (a) demonstration of stability, (b) teacher input, and (c) scheduling between consultants and teachers. Thus, this limitation is not a serious concern as baseline lengths were selected by teachers and consultants for applied reasons, as opposed to experimental reasons.

Process Validity

The primary purpose of the current manuscript is to demonstrate how practicing school psychologists can contribute to the empirical intervention science via the Non-Con M-B A-S design. Yet, the process used in the current study appears to lack social validity. Perhaps the biggest concern is that during consultation, consultant-consultee dyads typically develop interventions independently, depending upon the presenting problem and assessment data. Because the same strategies were used across cases, the consultation process used in the current study appears to have been contaminated.

In the current study, several variables contributed to different consultants using similar interventions across cases. First, in each case, referrals were for the same problem. Second, each of the consultants was a graduate student who had taken the same prerequisite courses in behavior analysis, behavioral consultation, and academic interventions. Third, for each consultation case, consultant-graduate students were required to locate experimental studies that supported the use of their interventions. Fourth, because the focus was on developing and implementing effective interventions, the consultants-graduate students were encouraged to combine components. Fifth, the consultant-graduate students were required to share case information and their results of research on empirically validated interventions. Finally, the consultant-graduate students were supervised by the same professor, who encouraged them to focus on increasing desirable behaviors, as opposed to decreasing undesirable behaviors.

While the teachers had final decision-making authority with respect to intervention development, the consulting graduate students obviously influenced this process. Some may feel that this compromises the process, thus decreasing the generalizability of the current demonstration to practitioners. However, it is unrealistic to think that consultants do not have an influence over intervention decisions. Furthermore, the entire process of empirically validating interventions is designed to encourage practitioners to use previous research to guide intervention development and implementation. This is exactly what the consultant-graduate students did in the current cases. Thus, the current demonstration has strong generalizability to practicing school psychologists who used previous consultation case experiences, training, and their exposure to empirical research to influence intervention selection across cases while consulting with educators (e.g., school psychologists following a scientist-practitioner model).

Another limitation with the Non-Con M-B A-S design is the possibility that from the pool of previous cases, only cases that work may be selected and included in the study. While this could occur given that professional journals rarely contain studies that suggest that a specific intervention did not appear to change behavior, this important issue is not limited to a specific design, but extends to the entire process of empirically validating interventions.

CONCLUSION

As with all applied studies, there are limitations associated with the current study that could be addressed by future researchers. Future researchers may be able to improve the science associated with the current study by conducting component analysis studies, collecting treatment integrity data, and holding intervention procedures more constant. However, even with these limitations, the current study does suggest that the intervention enhanced handwriting productivity across students, settings, and teacher-consultant dyads. Future researchers should continue to investigate these combined strategies and their effects on academic productivity in other subject areas, across students, and with intact classrooms (i.e., class-wide).

In the school psychology profession, there has been a recent focus on empirically validated interventions (Kratochwill & Stoiber, 2002). However, professional school psychology journals contain few reports of experimental intervention validation studies (Robinson et al., 1998). Yet, each day school psychologists are working with others (e.g., student assistant teams, consulting with teachers and parents) to develop, implement, and evaluate interventions designed to remedy student problems. Although the current study was conducted with University students and a faculty member, the current study demonstrates how *practicing school psychologists* who collect within-student, time-series data (e.g., school psychologists using BC) can combine data across non-concurrent cases and demonstrate experimental control using the Non-Con M-B A-S design. Through such cause-and-effect research, *practitioners* may be able to remedy students' presenting problems, while helping to develop a science of human behavior that they require to enhance their ability to prevent and remedy future problems.

NOTES

1. This manuscript was submitted to another journal and a anonymous reviewer indicated this concern. We would like to thank this unknown reviewer for their contribution, as this limitation did not occur to us.
2. If all variables that could affect behavior were known, the need for theoretical experimental research would be minimal.

REFERENCES

Baer, D. M., Wolf, M. M., & Risley, T. R. (1968). Some current dimensions of applied behavior analysis. *Journal of Applied Behavior Analysis, 1*, 91-97.
Barlow, D. H., & Hersen, M. (1984). *Single case experimental designs: Strategies for studying behavior change, 2nd Ed*. New York: Pergamon.

Bergan, J. R. (1977). *Behavioral Consultation.* New York: Charles E Merrill.

Bergan, J. R., & Kratochwill, T. R. (1990). *Behavioral consultation and therapy.* New York: Plenum Press.

Borasi, R., & Rose, B. J. (1989). Journal writing and mathematics instruction. *Educational Studies in Mathematics, 20,* 347-365.

Caldwell, N. K., Wolery, M., Werts, M. G., & Caldwell, Y. (1996). Embedding instructive feedback into teacher-student interactions during independent seat work. *Journal of Behavioral Education, 6,* 459-480.

Campbell, S., & Skinner, C. H. (2004). Combining explicit timing with an interdependent group contingency program to decrease transitions times: An investigation of the timely transitions game. *Journal of Applied School Psychology, 20*(2), 11-27.

Campbell, D. T., & Stanley, J. C. (1963). *Experimental and quasi-experimental designs for research.* Skokie, IL: Rand McNally.

Christenson, S. L., Thurlow, M. L., Ysseldyke, J.E., & McVicar, R. (1989). Written language instruction for students with mild handicaps: Is there enough quantity to ensure quality? *Learning Disability Quarterly, 12,* 219-229.

Daniels, L. K., & Hansen, K. P. (1976). Effects of social reinforcement and visual feedback on work production among mentally retarded sheltered workshop clients. *Psychological Reports, 39,* 664.

DiGangi, S. A., Maag, J. W., & Rutherford, R. B. (1991). Self-graphing of on-task behavior: Enhancing the reactive effects of self-monitoring on on-task behavior and academic performance. *Learning Disability Quarterly, 14,* 221-230.

Harris, F. N., & Jenson, W. R. (1985). Comparisons of multiple-baseline across persons designs and AB designs with replication: Issues and confusion. *Behavioral Assessment, 7,* 121-127.

Hayes, S. C. (1985). Natural multiple baseline across persons: A reply to Harris and Jenson. *Behavioral Assessment, 7,* 129-132.

Hoover, R. M. (1979). In the beginning: The word. *Journal of Basic Writing, 2,* 82-87.

Kazdin, A. E. (1974). Reactive self-monitoring: The effects of response desirability, goal setting, and feedback. *Journal of Consulting and Clinical Psychology, 422,* 704-706.

Kazdin, A. E. & Kopel, S. A. (1975). On resolving ambiguities of the multiple-baseline design: Problems and recommendations. *Behavior Therapy, 6,* 601-608.

Kelley, M. L., & Stokes, T. F. (1984). Student-teacher contracting with goal setting for maintenance. *Behavior Modification, 8,* 223-244.

Kratochwill, T. R., & Stoiber, K. C. (2002). Evidence-based interventions in school psychology: Conceptual foundations of the *Procedural and Coding Manual of Division 16 and the Society for the Study of School Psychology Task Force. School Psychology Quarterly, 17,* 341-389.

Lee, G., & Tindal, G. A. (1994). Self-recording and goal-setting: Effects on on-task and math productivity of low-achieving Korean elementary school students. *Journal of Behavioral Education, 4,* 459-479.

Maag, J. W., Rutherford, R. B., & DiGangi, S. A. (1992). Effects of self-monitoring and contingent reinforcement on on-task behavior and academic productivity of learning-disabled students: A social validation study. *Psychology in the Schools, 29,* 157-172.

McConnell, S. R. (1987). Entrapment effects and the generalization and maintenance of social skills training for elementary school students with behavioral disorders. *Behavioral Disorders, 12,* 252-263.

McLaughlin, T. (1992). Effects of written feedback in reading on behaviorally disordered students. *Journal of Educational Research, 85,* 312-316.

Moxley, R. A., Lutz, P. A., Ahlborn, P., Boley, N., & Armstrong, L. (1995). Self-recorded word counts of freewriting in grades 1-4. *Education and Treatment of Children, 18,* 139-157.

Neef, N. A., Shade, D., & Miller, M. S. (1994). Assessing influential dimensions of reinforcers on choice in students with serious emotional disturbance. *Journal of Applied Behavior Analysis, 27,* 575-583.

Rickards-Schlichting, K. A., Kehle, T. J., & Bray, M. A. (2004). A self-modeling intervention for high school students with public speaking anxiety. *Journal of Applied School Psychology, 20*(2), 47-60.

Robinson, S. L., Skinner, C. H., & Brown, C. S. (1998). An analysis of articles appearing in school psychology journals from 1985-1994. *Proven practices: Prevention and Remediation Solutions for Schools, 1,* 28-33.

Seabaugh, G. O., & Schumaker, J. B. (1994). The effects of self-regulation training on the academic productivity of secondary students with learning problems. *Journal of Behavioral Education, 4,* 109-133.

Shapiro, E. S. (1996). *Academic skills problems: Direct assessment and interventions.* New York: Guilford.

Shimabukro, S. M., Prater, M. A., Jenkins, A., & Edelen-Smith, P. (1999). The effects of self-monitoring of academic performance on students with learning disabilities and ADD/ADHD. *Education and Treatment of Children, 22,* 397-414.

Sindelar, P. T., Rosenberg, M. S., & Wilson, R. J. (1985). An adapted alternating treatments design for instructional researcher. *Education and Treatment of Children, 8,* 67-76.

Skinner, C. H. (2002). An empirical analysis of interspersal research: Evidence, implications, and applications for the discrete task completion hypothesis. *Journal of School Psychology, 40,* 347-368.

Stoiber, K. C., & Kratochwill, T. R. (2000). Empirically supported interventions and school psychology: Rationale and methodological issues-Part I. *School Psychology Quarterly, 15,* 75-105.

Stokes, T. R., & Baer, D. M. (1977). An implicit technology of generalization. *Journal of Applied Behavior Analysis, 10,* 349-367.

Trammel, D. L., Schloss, P. J., & Alper, S. (1994). Using self-recording, evaluation, and graphing to increase completion of homework assignments. *Journal of Learning Disabilities,* 75-81.

Watson, P. J., & Workman, E. A. (1981). The non-concurrent multiple baseline across-individuals design: An extension of the traditional multiple baseline design. *Journal of Behavior Therapy and Experimental Psychiatry, 12,* 257-259.

Young, K. R., West, R. P., Li, L., & Peterson, L. (1997). Teaching self-management skills to students with learning and behavior problems. *Journal of Emotional and Behavioral Problems, 6,* 90-96.

The Taped-Problems Intervention: Increasing Division Fact Fluency Using a Low-Tech Self-Managed Time-Delay Intervention

Elizabeth McCallum
Christopher H. Skinner
Holly Hutchins

University of Tennessee

SUMMARY. A multiple-probe across-tasks design was used to determine if the taped-problems intervention, a variation of the taped-words interventions (Freeman & McLaughlin, 1984), could be used to enhance division fact fluency in a fourth-grade student. During the taped-problems intervention, the student was given a list of problems on a sheet of paper and instructed to attempt to complete each problem before the answer was provided by an audiotape player. On the tapes, problems were read followed by their answers. Progressive time delay procedures were used as intervals between the problem and answer were adjusted. Initially, the interval between the problem being read and the answer was 1 second. During each session, as problems were repeated, the interval

---

Address correspondence to: Christopher H. Skinner, PhD, The University of Tennessee, College of EHHS, Claxton Complex A-518, Knoxville, TN 37996-3452 (E-mail: cskinne1@utk.edu).

[Haworth co-indexing entry note]: "The Taped-Problems Intervention: Increasing Division Fact Fluency Using a Low-Tech Self-Managed Time-Delay Intervention." McCallum, Elizabeth, Christopher H. Skinner, and Holly Hutchins. Co-published simultaneously in *Journal of Applied School Psychology* (The Haworth Press, Inc.) Vol. 20, No. 2, 2004, pp. 129-147; and: *Single-Subject Designs for School Psychologists* (ed: Christopher H. Skinner) The Haworth Press, Inc., 2004, pp. 129-147. Single or multiple copies of this article are available for a fee from The Haworth Document Delivery Service [1-800-HAWORTH, 9:00 a.m. - 5:00 p.m. (EST). E-mail address: docdelivery@haworthpress.com].

was gradually increased and then reduced. Results showed clear increases in division fact fluency after the intervention was implemented. This enhanced performance appeared to be maintained. Discussion focuses on future research related to the taped-problems intervention. *[Article copies available for a fee from The Haworth Document Delivery Service: 1-800-HAWORTH.   E-mail   address: <docdelivery@haworthpress.com> Website: <http://www.HaworthPress.com> © 2004 by The Haworth Press, Inc. All rights reserved.]*

KEYWORDS. Tape-problems, time-delay, math fluency, self-management, multiple-probe across-tasks design

Basic mathematics computation facts include solving simple (e.g., one-digit plus one-digit) addition, subtraction, multiplication, and division problems (Hasselbring, Goin, & Bradsford, 1987). Because basic computation skills are necessary for completing more complex computation problems, it may not be sufficient for students to merely acquire the ability to solve these problems; they should also be able to arrive at the correct answer *rapidly* (Deno & Mirkin, 1978; Haring & Eaton, 1978; Shapiro, 1996). Fluency, automaticity, and proficiency are terms often used to describe rapid and accurate responding (Hasselbring et al.,1987; Haring & Eaton, 1978; Shapiro, 1996).

Those who can complete basic facts automatically may have more cognitive resources available to apply to learning more complex computation algorithms or concepts (LaBerge & Samuels, 1974; Wong, 1986). Additionally, the more rapidly students can complete the basic mathematics facts, the more quickly they can complete complex items (Skinner, Fletcher, & Henington, 1996). Thus, they receive more opportunities to practice these complex items, which can enhance generalization and discrimination skills (Skinner & Schock, 1995). Finally, those who can complete basic facts both rapidly and accurately may find complex mathematics tasks less frustrating and have lower levels of mathematics anxiety than those who can not complete basic facts automatically (Cates & Rhymer, 2003).

Numerous procedures have been used to increase automaticity with basic math facts (Greenwood, Delquadri, & Hall, 1989; Rhymer, Dittmer, Skinner, & Jackson, 2000; Skinner, Turco, Beatty, & Rasavage, 1989). Perhaps the most important shared characteristic of these procedures is that they occasion high rates of active, accurate responding (Greenwood,

Delquadri, & Hall, 1984). Researchers have compared interventions and shown that interventions that occasion higher rates of accurate academic responding result in greater increases in fluency than those that occasion lower rates of responding (Skinner, Bamberg, Smith, & Powell, 1993; Skinner, Belfiore, Mace, Williams, & Johns, 1997).

TAPED WORDS INTERVENTIONS

An intervention that has been used to enhance rapid, accurate sight-word reading is the taped-words intervention (Freeman & McLaughlin, 1984). During this intervention, audiotapes are constructed that provide words in the same sequence as lists. Students are provided with the lists and instructed to read the lists along with the tape. Results have shown that this procedure is effective for enhancing word list reading fluency (i.e., words correct per minute on word lists).

In Freeman and McLaughlin's study (1984), the audiotapes presented words at a rapid rate (80 words per minute) because neurological impress or modeling theories (Cunningham, 1979; Heckelman, 1969) suggested that rapid rates of presentation may enhance students' reading rates. Subsequent studies confirmed the effectiveness of the taped words intervention (Shapiro & McCurdy, 1989; Skinner, Johnson, Larkin, Lessley, & Glowacki, 1995; Skinner & Shapiro, 1989; Skinner, Smith, & McLean, 1994; Sterling, Robinson, & Skinner, 1997). However, in these studies, researchers altered word presentation rates or implemented experimental procedures designed to control for opportunities to respond embedded within the taped-words intervention. Results from these studies suggest that neither neurological impress nor students' modeling the rapid pace of the tape accounted for the increases in students' accurate reading rates. Rather, these studies suggested that the opportunities to respond embedded within the intervention and provided during assessment procedures caused the increases in reading fluency.

TIME DELAY

Time delay procedures have been used to enhance accurate responding with individuals with various degrees of learning disabilities and mental retardation (Ault, Wolery, Doyle, & Gast, 1989). Two types of time delay procedures, constant and progressive time delay, have been used to enhance accurate responding. Both include multiple trials consisting of (a) the presentation of an antecedent stimulus, (b) an interval for students to respond to that antecedent stimulus, and (c) an additional stimulus or prompt that follows the antecedent stimulus when students fail to respond accurately. Table 1 depicts this process and provides examples of how the process would work when students fail to respond within the response interval, respond inaccurately within the response interval, and respond accurately within the response interval.

With time delay, the goal is to have the student respond accurately to the antecedent stimulus. Thus, for a division fact, an antecedent stimulus may be a printed problem (i.e., 42/7 = __). Following the presentation of the antecedent stimulus, an interval is provided for the student to respond. If the student emits a correct response during this interval, then this response is typically followed by reinforcement or praise (see Table 1, example 3). If the student responds inaccurately or fails to respond during the designated interval, an additional artificial prompt(s) is provided that is designed to occasion an accurate response (see Table 1, examples 1 and 2). For a division fact this additional prompt may merely be stating the problem with the correct answer (e.g., the teacher says "42/7 = 6").

Time delay procedures provide students with an opportunity to *independently* respond to the initial antecedent stimuli (e.g., 42/7 = __). However, when students fail to respond or emit inaccurate responses to the natural antecedent stimuli, the additional artificial prompts are designed to occasion subsequent accurate responses. Thus, all trials typi-

TABLE 1. Graphic Depiction of a Constant Time Delay Procedure with 5 Second Response Intervals and Examples of Procedure When Student Fails to Respond Within 5 Seconds (i.e., 1), Responds Inaccurately Within 5 Seconds (i.e., 2), and Responds Accurately Within the 5 Second Response Interval.

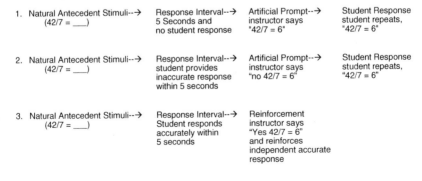

1. Natural Antecedent Stimuli--→ (42/7 = ___)	Response Interval--→ 5 Seconds and no student response	Artificial Prompt--→ instructor says "42/7 = 6"	Student Response student repeats, "42/7 = 6"
2. Natural Antecedent Stimuli--→ (42/7 = ___)	Response Interval--→ student provides inaccurate response within 5 seconds	Artificial Prompt--→ instructor says "no 42/7 = 6"	Student Response student repeats, "42/7 = 6"
3. Natural Antecedent Stimuli--→ (42/7 = ___)	Response Interval--→ Student responds accurately within 5 seconds	Reinforcement instructor says "Yes 42/7 = 6" and reinforces independent accurate response	

cally involve one correct response and the student's last response is almost always an accurate response.

Initially students may fail to respond accurately to the natural antecedent stimuli. However, after repeated trials, students often begin responding correctly to the natural antecedent stimuli prior to the delivery of the artificial prompts. Thus, stimulus control is transferred from accurate responding to the artificial prompts to accurate responding to the naturally occurring antecedent stimulus. Now the student is independently emitting desired responses to naturally occurring stimuli.

When using *constant time delay* the time provided for students to respond independently (i.e., interval between the natural antecedent stimuli and artificial prompt) remains constant across trials. Although constant time delay procedures are abundant in the literature, only the second type of time delay, *progressive time delay*, was chosen for integration into the present intervention. Progressive time delay procedures involve providing progressively shorter or longer intervals between a stimulus and a response (Wolery, Ault, Doyle, & Gast, 1986). For example, the stimulus is shown and an individual has a very brief amount of time to respond. As time delay trials continue, this time interval is gradually increased, allowing more time for responses. When the time delay is brief, students have little time to respond before the prompt is delivered. Thus, initially a no-time delay condition can prevent students from making errors. Gradually increasing the delay during subsequent trials then allows students to respond independently, before the artificial prompt is delivered.

In contrast, time delay trials can begin with large delays that are gradually decreased. The large delays may increase errors, but also provide students with more time to independently emit accurate responses to the naturally occurring stimuli (McCurdy, Cundari, & Lentz, 1990; Wolery, Ault, Doyle, & Gast, 1986). Gradually reducing delays then can be used to occasion automatic responding.

Progressive time delay procedures have been used effectively in promoting various tasks with various populations. McCurdy, Cundari, and Lentz (1990) found a progressive time delay procedure to be more effective in teaching sight words to students with behavior disorders than both direct instruction and observational learning. Similarly, Browder, Hines, McCarthy, and Fees (1984) successfully used a progressive time delay procedure to teach sight-word recognition and daily living skills such as answering telephones and doing laundry to a group of adults with severe handicaps. Progressive time delay procedures also have been used effectively in teaching language skills (Halle, Marshall, &

Spradlin, 1979), food preparation (Schuster, Gast, Wolery, & Guiltinan, 1988), and banking skills (McDonnell & Ferguson, 1989). Most of these studies have been conducted with students with moderate or severe handicaps.

Purpose

The current study was conducted to determine if the taped-words intervention could be adapted to address mathematics division fact fluency deficits. In the current study, each basic division fact was presented four or five times. Rather than being encouraged to respond with the tape (see Freeman & McLaughlin, 1984), students were asked to try to write the correct math fact answer *before* it was provided on the tape.

In addition to altering the target skill, we adapted the taped-words procedure by employing progressive time delays in an attempt to occasion higher rates of accurate academic responding. In the current study we employed both forms of progressive time delay. In an attempt to reduce error rates, initially each problem was presented on the tape with a brief time interval or delay (e.g, 1-second) between the problem being read and the answer being read. These intervals were then increased (e.g., 5-seconds) to provide opportunities for independent responding (e.g., responding before the answers were read on the tape). This also allowed students to use the audio cues as feedback to reinforce accurate independent responding and prompt error correction when responses were inaccurate (Skinner, Turco et al., 1989). Intervals were then decreased to encourage more rapid or automatic responding.

METHOD

Student and Setting

Peter, a 10-year-old male African-American student from a general education fourth-grade classroom was referred by his teacher because he had fallen behind his classmates in math class, particularly with regard to simple division. His teacher indicated that Peter was a good student but that he often used a finger-counting procedure while doing his division. While this procedure allowed Peter to arrive at accurate answers, he was unable to complete his assignments or tests quickly enough to receive passing grades.

The current study was conducted in an unassigned classroom in Peter's school that was used for various purposes on an *as needed* basis. During the sessions, the researcher(s) and Peter were alone in the room. Activities were conducted at a table with the primary researcher seated next to Peter.

Materials

A tape recorder, headphones, and stopwatch were used throughout this experiment. Baseline and intervention data were collected via experimenter-constructed division fact probes. Basic division facts 2-9 were divided into three sets (see Table 2) of 22, 21, and 21 problems respectively. Multiples of one and inversion facts (i.e., either $12 \div 4$ or $12 \div 3$ but not both) were excluded from the probes.

Three audiotapes were made, one for each of the three sets of problems. Tapes were constructed for each set by reading the 22 or 21 prob-

TABLE 2. The Three Sets of Division Problems.

Set A	Set B	Set C
$9 \div 3$	$24 \div 6$	$48 \div 6$
$28 \div 7$	$12 \div 2$	$14 \div 2$
$16 \div 8$	$72 \div 8$	$56 \div 8$
$54 \div 6$	$21 \div 3$	$15 \div 3$
$16 \div 4$	$20 \div 4$	$36 \div 4$
$40 \div 5$	$36 \div 9$	$72 \div 9$
$10 \div 2$	$18 \div 2$	$8 \div 2$
$5 \div 5$	$15 \div 5$	$35 \div 5$
$64 \div 8$	$12 \div 3$	$6 \div 3$
$27 \div 3$	$45 \div 5$	$20 \div 5$
$54 \div 9$	$56 \div 7$	$63 \div 7$
$28 \div 4$	$48 \div 8$	$32 \div 8$
$18 \div 3$	$63 \div 9$	$45 \div 9$
$27 \div 9$	$24 \div 8$	$12 \div 4$
$36 \div 6$	$42 \div 6$	$30 \div 6$
$4 \div 2$	$6 \div 2$	$42 \div 7$
$49 \div 7$	$32 \div 4$	$24 \div 4$
$40 \div 8$	$35 \div 7$	$18 \div 9$
$81 \div 9$	$30 \div 5$	$12 \div 6$
$10 \div 5$	$14 \div 7$	$24 \div 3$
$18 \div 6$	$8 \div 4$	$21 \div 7$
$16 \div 2$		

lems and their answers into the tape four or five times. Problems were numbered and the number of the problem was read immediately preceding the reading of the problem. The order of problems was randomly sequenced for each of the readings.

Originally, all three tapes were constructed in the same manner based on a progressive time delay format. Specifically, the series of 22 or 21 problems was read the first time through with no time delay between the answer and problem. The second series was read with a 3-second time delay between reading the problem and giving the answer. The third series was read with a 5-second time delay between reading the problems and then reading the answers. The final two readings included 2- and 1-second delays, respectively. Thus, each problem and answer was read 5 times. For each series problem order was randomized.

While working on Set A, Peter complained about the long delay on the middle series. Therefore, for sets B and C new tapes were constructed where the 5-second time delay series was removed, leaving only four readings per tape: no delay, 3-second, 2-second, and 1-second delays. The interval between reading the answer to one problem and reading the next problem remained 3 seconds across all three tapes.

Intervention worksheets were constructed for each tape. These worksheets contained each problem and a space to write the answer (e.g., $42 \div 6 =$ ____). Problems were provided on the worksheets in the same sequence as on the tape.

Three different assessment sheets were also constructed for each set of problems. Assessment sheets contained the 21 or 22 problems with spaces provided for answers. The problems were randomly sequenced across sheets.

Dependent Measures, Experimental Design, and Conditions

A multiple-probe-across-tasks (i.e., sets of problems) design was used to evaluate the effects of the intervention (Cuvo, 1979; Horner & Baer, 1978). Percent correct and digits correct per minute were the dependent measures used in this study. Both were measured during 1-minute timed assessment probes. Percent correct was calculated by dividing the number of correct answers by the total number of problems answered and multiplying by 100. Unanswered problems were not scored when calculating accuracy.

Deno and Mirkin's (1977) scoring procedure was used to calculate digits correct per minute (DCM) for each assessment probe. To be scored as correct, a correct digit had to be written in the correct place. Thus for the problem 132 ÷ 11 = ____, an answer of 12 would have been scored as 2-digits correct because both correct digits are in the correct place. An answer of 22, 15, or 1 would have been scored as 1-digit correct and answer of 21 or 55 would have been scored as 0 digits correct. When Peter finished all the problems on an assessment probe before the minute was over, the number of seconds he took to complete the probe was recorded. Digits correct per minute were calculated by totaling digits correct, dividing by the number of seconds it took Peter to complete the probe, and multiplying by 60.

Procedures

Each day at 9:30 AM the primary experimenter entered the empty classroom and set up materials. She then escorted Peter from his classroom and seated him at the table in the experimental room.

Assessment Procedure: Baseline, Probes, and Intervention. During the first three sessions, assessment procedures were run for each set of problems. The experimenter used a stopwatch to time each assessment for 1 minute. Peter was given the assessment probes one at a time in random order. Peter was directed to complete as many problems as he could in 1 minute. When the first minute was up, Peter was instructed to put his pencil down and wait for the next assessment sheet. No performance feedback was given. Following the initial three baseline sessions, Peter's performance on the target set (i.e., the set of items being addressed with the taped-problems intervention) was assessed each session. The non-target sets were not assessed each day. Instead assessments for these items were probed (i.e., administered prior to the implementation of a new list). This intermittent assessment procedure was used to decrease the probability of Peter becoming frustrated by having to work on problems that were not being targeted during the current intervention phase (Cuvo, 1979). Probe procedures also allowed for the collection of maintenance data.

Intervention Phases: Taped-Problems Intervention. Following the third baseline session, the first intervention session was run with Problem Set A. After the assessment, Peter was given a follow-along packet for the Set A tape. The packet listed the problems in the numbered order that they would be heard on the tape. Peter was given a blank sheet of paper with which to cover the problems below the particular problem being read. Peter was told to use this paper to help him stay with the tape and not skip ahead.

Peter was told that he was going to listen to a tape-recorder. He was instructed to look at his intervention packet and follow along with the tape that would supply the problems and answers. He was instructed to try to write the answer to each problem following its reading but before the reading of the answer. Thus, he was encouraged to try to beat the tape. When he wrote an incorrect response, Peter was instructed to write a slash on the incorrect answer and write the correct response as heard on the tape. If he failed to beat the tape, he was instructed to write the correct answer after its reading. After Peter indicated that he understood the instructions, he was told to put on the headphones and press the 'play' button to begin. When he finished the intervention sheets, he was instructed to stop the tape.

Following the tape, Peter was given another assessment probe for the specific problem set he was working on. This probe was randomly selected, with one exception; the probe given during the pre-intervention assessment was excluded from the selection process. The same timing procedures used during baseline were used with this probe. Data from probes following intervention sessions (listening to the tapes) were not used as the dependent variable for this study. Instead, this assessment probe was designed to allow Peter the opportunity to independently practice items just drilled. Following the first intervention session, each session included (a) assessment procedures, used to collect data for the dependent variable, (b) the taped-problems intervention, and (c) another assessment to allow Peter to practice problems he had just been exposed to. Thus dependent variable assessment probes occurred between 24, 48, or 72 (weekends and absences) hours after the intervention sessions.

After Peter demonstrated improved performance with one set of problems, the tape was switched and similar procedures were run with subsequent tapes. On most days, before beginning the taped-problems intervention, assessment procedures were run for only the set targeted. However, after Peter achieved stability on one set of items, the following day assessments were conducted for all three sets of problems (multiple-probes, see Cuvo, 1979) and the intervention for the subsequent set was implemented. On the last session, all three sets were again assessed to check for maintenance of set A and B items.

In order to enhance cooperation, each day Peter earned a star on a calendar for following directions throughout the intervention phase. After receiving 4 stars, his teacher allowed him to choose a "treasure" (pencil, stickers, etc.) from her class "treasure box." Peter earned a star each day. Additionally, during each session Peter was praised for trying his best. However, no mathematics performance-based feedback or rewards were delivered during this study.

Interobserver Agreement and Procedural Integrity

A second observer sat in the room approximately 8 feet from the table and collected procedural integrity data during five of the 15 (33%) intervention sessions. During these intervention sessions, the independent observer recorded the presence or absence of 21 experimenter behaviors (see Table 3). Results showed 100% integrity. Additionally, during a baseline session, the observer recorded the experimenter completing steps 1-7 three consecutive times and step 21 at the end of the session. These data suggest strong procedural integrity.

The second experimenter also independently scored digits correct for one baseline session and these five intervention sessions (13 or 34% of the probes). Interscorer agreement was calculated by dividing the num-

TABLE 3. The Treatment Integrity Checklist.

1. _____ Place probe face-down in front of student.
2. _____ Set timer to zero.
3. _____ Instruct student to turn paper over and begin working.
4. _____ Start timer.
5. _____ When timer reaches 1 minute, say "time's up" and stop timer.
6. _____ Collect probe.
7. _____ If student finishes before 1 minute, write exact time at top of probe.
8. _____ Give student headphones and appropriate Follow-Along sheet.
9. _____ Instruct student to keep up with tape but not to work ahead.
10. _____ When student is ready, start tape.
11. _____ When tape ends, collect Follow-Along sheet.
12. _____ Repeat assessment procedures with set of problems.
13. _____ Place probe face-down in front of student.
14. _____ Set timer to zero.
15. _____ Instruct student to turn paper over and begin working.
16. _____ Start timer.
17. _____ When timer reaches 1 minute, say "time's up" and stop timer.
18. _____ Collect probe.
19. _____ If student finishes before 1 minute, write exact time at top of probe.
20. _____ Give student a star on corresponding date on calendar.
21. _____ Escort student back to classroom with no performance feedback delivered.

ber of agreements on digits correct by the number of agreements plus disagreements and multiplying by 100. Interscorer agreement on digits correct was 100%. Finally, this independent observer also recorded the number of seconds the student spent working on assessment across the same 13 assessments. The two observers recorded the identical number of seconds for all 13 assessments.

RESULTS

Figure 1 displays the percentage of accurate completed problems per minute for the student during baseline and intervention phases. Figure 1 confirms teacher reports indicating that Peter's division accuracy was high prior to implementing the intervention. These high levels of accuracy prevent us from drawing conclusions regarding the intervention's impact on this dependent variable.

Figure 2 displays the data on digits correct per minute across conditions and sets of problems. During baseline, Peter's digits correct per minute for each set were fairly stable. Baseline digits correct per minute ranged between 11-16 for set A and 7-13 for set B. Baseline performance on Set C appeared to contain one outlier during the first probe session (session 7) where he only got 3 digits correct per minute. Excluding this data point, baseline digits correct per minute on set C ranged from 10-18.

For all three sets of lists, Peter showed a rapid increase in digits correct per minute after the intervention was applied. Mean digits correct per minute for sets A, B, and C increased from 13 to 26, 10 to 25, and 12 to 28 respectively. Additionally, data show that after three intervention sessions Peter appeared to reach a ceiling, with little or no additional improvement in digits correct per minute. The maintenance checks completed on the last session for Sets A and B showed that Peter's enhanced fluency was maintained over time (12 days for set A, 7 days for set B).

DISCUSSION

Previous researchers have shown that the taped-words intervention is an effective procedure for enhancing word list reading fluency (e.g., Freeman & McLaughlin, 1984; Shapiro & McCurdy, 1989). In the current study, we modified the taped-words procedures to target division fact fluency and incorporated two forms of progressive time delay pro-

FIGURE 1. Percent Correct of Problems Completed Across Conditions

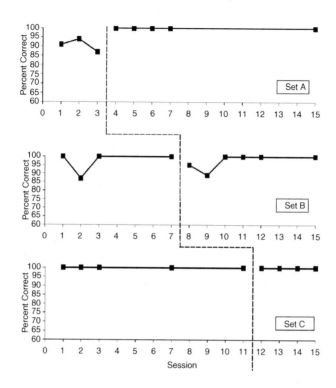

cedures. Results showed rapid increases in digits correct per minute across sets of problems following the application of the taped-problems procedure. Additionally, data from Sets A and B suggest that enhanced fluency was maintained. These data suggest that the taped-problems intervention was successful in increasing Peter's division fact fluency.

While the data suggest that the taped-problems procedure was effective, future research on this intervention is needed. Researchers should assess the external validity of the taped-problem interventions by running similar procedures across students (e.g., students with learning disabilities) and tasks (e.g., multiplication problems). Prior to the intervention, Peter used a finger-counting procedure to reliably, but slowly, arrive at correct answers. Future researchers should assess the effects of the taped-problems procedure with students who are currently responding in-

FIGURE 2. Digits Correct per Minute Across Conditions

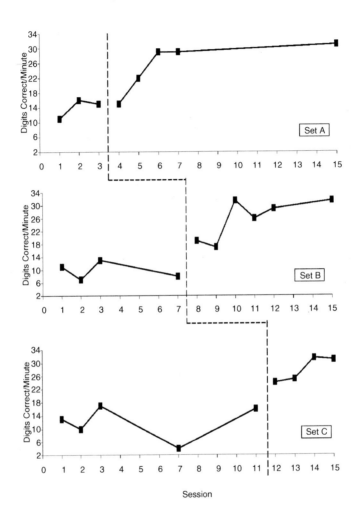

Session

accurately to problems and/or have not developed such strategies to solve problems.

Although researchers were present throughout the intervention, the taped-problems intervention is designed so that students need little if any assistance implementing the intervention. Thus, future researchers should also conduct studies under conditions that may be more reflective of typical educational environments. For example, future researchers should determine if the taped-problems intervention would be effective when used with an entire class or in learning centers where students work independently.

During the current study, we employed a progressive time delay procedure, starting with a brief delay, increasing the delay, and then decreasing the delay. The initial brief interval (i.e., 1-second) between the problem and answer being delivered prevented Peter from using his count-by procedure to arrive at correct answers. The increase in delay was designed to allow Peter to respond independently and use the tape for feedback. Subsequent decreases were used to encourage rapid responding. Future researchers should alter the time delay procedures to determine which procedures are most effective and to determine if specific procedures are more effective depending upon students' level of skill development.

In the current study, Peter reported that he did not like the 5-second delay condition. Thus, we altered the tapes by eliminating this long delay series for Sets B and C. This suggests that future researchers should assess student acceptability with different time delay procedures (Turco & Elliott, 1986). Because students may be less likely to implement an intervention that they find unacceptable (Skinner & Smith, 1992), these acceptability studies may prove critical for developing taped-problems procedures that are self-managed in learning centers or similar situations (e.g., class-wide). Additionally, more advanced technologies (e.g., computers and software) may be used to alter time delays on an item-by-item basis as student responding improves.

Researchers have found that rate of word presentation during the taped-words intervention may impact learning. Specifically, in some instances the longer the delay between word presentations, the greater number of words learned. However, because this procedure lengthened the time required to complete the intervention, actual learning rates were depressed when the intervals between words were increased (Skinner, Belfiore, & Watson, 1995/2002). In the current study, when the 5-second delay series was eliminated on tapes for Sets B and C, the number of opportunities to respond decreased by 20%. However, the data suggest that this reduction had little impact on increases in fluency (i.e., had little impact on learning levels). Additionally, the time required to run the intervention was decreased by over 30% (a decrease of over 3 minutes). Thus, learning rates were higher for sets B and C when the long series was eliminated. Future researchers should conduct studies where both the time delay and the number of opportunities to respond are manipulated to determine procedures that result in the greatest increase in learning rates.

In the current study, Peter wrote his responses. Thus, new intervention packets with problems were required for each session. Future researchers should determine if altering the taped-problems response to a verbal or sub-vocal response would be equally, or more effective (Skinner, Bamberg, Smith, & Powell, 1993; Skinner, Belfiore, Mace, Williams, & Johns, 1997), as such procedures would take less time and reduce the need to prepare multiple packets that allow students to provide written response.

In the current study, assessment procedures were run to provide Peter an opportunity to independently practice items following the taped-problems intervention. Researchers should conduct component analysis studies to determine the degree to which these procedures enhanced the effectiveness of the intervention.

CONCLUSION

School psychologists have been charged with preventing and remedying student problems through the application of empirically validated interventions (Kratochwill & Stoiber, 2002; Stoiber & Kratochwill, 2000). The current study showed that the taped-problems intervention was an effective procedure for enhancing division fact fluency. School psychologists should continue to contribute to the development of more effective interventions by conducting future research on the taped-problems intervention designed to assess the external validity of this intervention and enhance the effectiveness and efficiency of the taped-problems procedure.

REFERENCES

Ault, M. J., Wolery, M., Doyle, P. M., & Gast, D. L. (1989). Review of comparative studies in the instruction of students with moderate and severe handicaps. *Exceptional Children, 55,* 346-356.

Browder, D. M., Hines, C., McCarthy, L. J. & Fees, J. (1984). A treatment package for increasing sight-word recognition for use in daily living skills. *Education and Training of the Mentally Retarded, 19,* 191-200.

Cates, G. L., & Rhymer, K. N. (2003). Examining the relationship between mathematics anxiety and mathematics performance. An instructional hierarchy perspective. *Journal of Behavioral Education, 12,* 23-34.

Cunningham, J. W. (1979). An automatic pilot for decoding. *The Reading Teacher, 32,* 420-424.

Cuvo, A. J. (1979). Multiple-baseline design in instructional research: Pitfalls of measurement and procedural advantages. *American Journal of Mental Deficiency, 84,* 219-228.

Deno, S. L., & Mirkin, P. K. (1977). *Data-based program modification: A manual.* Reston, VA: Council for Exceptional Children.

Freeman, T. J., & McLaughlin, T. F. (1984). Effects of a taped-words treatment procedure on learning disabled students' sight-word reading. *Learning Disability Quarterly, 7,* 49-54.

Greenwood, C. R., Delquadri, J., & Hall, R. V. (1984). Opportunity to respond and student academic performance. In W. L. Heward, T. E. Heron, J. Trap-Porter, & D. S. Hill (Eds.), *Focus on behavior analysis in education* (pp. 58-88). Columbus, OH: Charles Merrill.

Greenwood, C. R., Delquadri, J., & Hall, R. V. (1989). Longitudinal effects of classwide peer tutoring. *Journal of Educational Psychology, 81,* 371-383.

Halle, J. W., Marshall, A. M., & Spradlin, J. E. (1979). Time delay: A technique to increase language use and facilitate generalization in retarded children. *Journal of Applied Behavior Analysis, 12,* 431-439.

Haring, N. G., & Eaton, M. D. (1978). Systematic instructional procedures: An instructional hierarchy. In N. G. Haring, T. C. Lovitt, M. D. Eaton, & C. L. Hansen (Eds.). *The fourth R: Research in the classroom* (pp. 23-40). Columbus, OH: Merrill.

Hasselbring, T. S., Goin, L. I. & Bradsford, J. D. (1987). Developing automaticity. *Teaching Exceptional Children, 1,* 30-33.

Heckelman, R. G. (1969). A neurological-impress method of remedial-reading instruction. *Academic Therapy, 5,* 277-282.

Horner, D. R., & Baer, D. M. (1978). Multiple-probe technique: A variation of the multiple-baseline. *Journal of Applied Behavior Analysis, 11,* 189-196.

Kratochwill, T. R., & Stoiber, K. C. (2002). Evidence-based interventions in school psychology: Conceptual foundations of the *Procedural and Coding Manual of Division 16 and the Society for the Study of School Psychology Task Force. School Psychology Quarterly, 17,* 341-389.

LaBerge, D., & Samuels, S. J. (1974). Toward a theory of automatic processing in reading. *Cognitive Psychology, 6,* 293-323.

McCurdy, B. L., Cundari, L., & Lentz, F. E. (1990). Enhancing instructional efficiency: An examination of time delay and the opportunity to observe instruction. *Education and Treatment of Children, 13,* 226-238.

McDonnell, J., & Ferguson, B. (1989). A comparison of time delay and decreasing prompt hierarchy strategies in teaching banking skills to students with moderate handicaps. *Journal of Applied Behavior Analysis, 22,* 85-91.

Rhymer, K. N., Dittmer, K. L., Skinner, C. H., & Jackson, B. (2000). Combining explicit timing, peer-delivered immediate feedback, positive-practice overcorrection and performance feedback to increase multiplication fluency. *School Psychology Quarterly, 15,* 40-51.

Schuster, J. W., Gast, D. L., Wolery, M., & Guiltinan, S. (1988). The effectiveness of a constant time-delay procedure to teach chained responses to adolescents with mental retardation. *Journal of Applied Behavior Analysis, 21*, 169-178.

Shapiro, E. S. (1996). *Academic skills problems: Direct assessment and intervention* (2nd ed.). New York: Guilford Press.

Shapiro, E. S. & McCurdy, B. L. (1989). Effects of a taped-words treatment on reading proficiency. *Exceptional Children, 55*, 321-325.

Skinner, C. H., Bamberg, H., Smith, E. S., & Powell, S. (1993). Subvocal responding to increase division fact fluency. *Remedial and Special Education, 14*, 49-56.

Skinner, C. H., Belfiore, P. B., & Watson, T. S. (1995/2002). Assessing the relative effects of interventions in students with mild disabilities: Assessing instructional time. *Journal of Psychoeducational Assessment, 20*, 345-356.15. (Reprinted from *Assessment in Rehabilitation and Exceptionality, 2*, 207-220, 1995).

Skinner, C. H., Belfiore, P. J., Mace, H. W., Williams, S., & Johns, G. A. (1997). Altering response topography to increase response efficiency and learning rates. *School Psychology Quarterly, 12*, 54-64.

Skinner, C. H., Fletcher, P. A., & Henington, C. (1996). Increasing learning trial rates by increasing student response rates. *School Psychology Quarterly, 11*, 313-325.

Skinner, C. H., Johnson, C. W., Larkin, M. J., Lessley, D. J., & Glowacki, M. L. (1995). The influence of rate of presentation during taped-words interventions on reading performance. *Journal of Emotional and Behavioral Disorders, 3*, 214-223.

Skinner, C. H., & Schock, H. H. (1995). Best practices in mathematics assessment. In A. Thomas & J. Grimes (Eds.), *Best practices in school psychology (3rd ed)* (pp. 731-740). Washington, D.C.: National Association of School Psychologists.

Skinner, C. H., & Shapiro, E. S. (1989). A comparison of a taped-words and drill interventions on reading fluency in adolescents with behavior disorders. *Education and Treatment of Children, 12*, 123-133.

Skinner, C. H., & Smith, E. S. (1992). Issues surrounding the use of self-managed interventions for increasing academic performance. *School Psychology Review, 21*, 202-210.

Skinner, C. H., Smith, E. S., & McLean, J. E. (1994). The effects of intertrial interval duration on sight-word learning during constant time delay. *Behavioral Disorders, 19*, 98-107.

Skinner, C. H., Turco, T. L., Beatty, K. L., & Rasavage, C. (1989). Cover, copy, and compare: An intervention for increasing multiplication performance. *School Psychology Review, 18*, 212-220.

Sterling, H. E., Robinson, S. L., & Skinner, C. H. (1997). The effects of two taped-words interventions on sight-word reading in students with mental retardation. *Journal of Behavior Education, 7*, 25-32.

Stoiber, K. C., & Kratochwill, T. R. (2000). Empirically supported interventions and school psychology: Rationale and methodological issues-Part I. *School Psychology Quarterly, 15*, 75-105.

Turco, T. L., & Elliott, S. N. (1986). Assessment of students' acceptability ratings of teacher-initiated interventions for classroom misbehavior. *Journal of School Psychology, 24*, 277-283.

Wolery, M., Ault, M. J., Doyle, P. M., & Gast, D. L. (1986). *Comparison of instructional strategies: A literature review.* Lexington, KY: University of Kentucky Press.

Wong, B. Y. L. (1986). Problems and issues in definition of learning disabilities. In J. K. Torgesen & B. Y. L. Wong (Eds.), *Psychological and educational perspectives on learning disabilities* (pp. 3-26). New York: Academic Press.

Index

BOOK ORDER FORM!

Order a copy of this book with this form or online at:
http://www.haworthpress.com/store/product.asp?sku=5517

Single-Subject Designs for School Psychologists

_____ in softbound at $24.95 (ISBN: 0-7890-2826-3)
_____ in hardbound at $39.95 (ISBN: 0-7890-2825-5)

COST OF BOOKS _____

POSTAGE & HANDLING _____
US: $4.00 for first book & $1.50
for each additional book
Outside US: $5.00 for first book
& $2.00 for each additional book.

SUBTOTAL _____

In Canada: add 7% GST._____

STATE TAX _____
CA, IL, IN, MN, NJ, NY, OH & SD residents
please add appropriate local sales tax.

FINAL TOTAL _____
If paying in Canadian funds, convert
using the current exchange rate,
UNESCO coupons welcome.

❏BILL ME LATER:
Bill-me option is good on US/Canada/
Mexico orders only; not good to jobbers,
wholesalers, or subscription agencies.

❏ Signature _____

❏ Payment Enclosed: $ _____

❏ PLEASE CHARGE TO MY CREDIT CARD:

❏Visa ❏MasterCard ❏AmEx ❏Discover
❏Diner's Club ❏Eurocard ❏ JCB

Account # _____

Exp Date _____

Signature _____
(Prices in US dollars and subject to change without notice.)

PLEASE PRINT ALL INFORMATION OR ATTACH YOUR BUSINESS CARD		
Name		
Address		
City	State/Province	Zip/Postal Code
Country		
Tel	Fax	
E-Mail		

May we use your e-mail address for confirmations and other types of information? ❏Yes ❏No We appreciate receiving
your e-mail address. Haworth would like to e-mail special discount offers to you, as a preferred customer.
We will never share, rent, or exchange your e-mail address. We regard such actions as an invasion of your privacy.

Order From Your **Local Bookstore** or Directly From
The Haworth Press, Inc. 10 Alice Street, Binghamton, New York 13904-1580 • USA
Call Our toll-free number (1-800-429-6784) / Outside US/Canada: (607) 722-5857
Fax: 1-800-895-0582 / Outside US/Canada: (607) 771-0012
E-mail your order to us: orders@haworthpress.com

For orders outside US and Canada, you may wish to order through your local
sales representative, distributor, or bookseller.
For information, see http://haworthpress.com/distributors

(Discounts are available for individual orders in US and Canada only, not booksellers/distributors.)

Please photocopy this form for your personal use.
www.HaworthPress.com

BOF05